Bloody Sunset
in
St. Augustine

A True Story

By
Nancy Powell and Jim Mast

Published by

D1566970

F ederal Point Publishing, Inc.
Rt. 2 Box 177-A East Palatka, Florida 32131

ISBN   0-9668259-0-X

Cover Design by Linda Barfield

*Photographs of Athalia Ponsell Lindsley on front and back cover
provided by her late husband James Lindsley.*

Photograph of St. Augustine Bridge of Lions and Skyline
St. Augustine Record *photo by Ralph D. Priddy.*

Published by

ederal Point Publishing, Inc.
Rt. 2 Box 177-A East Palatka, Florida 32131

ISBN   0-9668259-0-X

Printed in USA by:
Brut Printing
503 Parker Street
Jacksonville, Florida. 32202

Dedication

For the memory of my husband, Edward, our youngest son, David Eric, and our granddaughter, Alyssa Madison Powell.

Also for all the Campbell and Powell children, grandchildren, and great-grandchildren---especially my granddaughter, Shannon Campbell Sellers.

Nancy Smith Powell---1998

~ ~ ~

For my wife Shirley, a very special lady ... .

And for our children; Kim, Joe, Mark and Kirk.

And for our grandchildren; Jackie, Jessica, Clay, Jenni, Jarod, Joshua, Eva and Jacob.

~~ Remember me.

Jim Mast---1998

TABLE OF CONTENTS

INTRODUCTION

Early in 1974 the nation's oldest and most bizarre city was imposed upon by a bloody and passionate murder which happened in the waning hours of daylight on a well-traveled street.

This is the story of how a newspaper reporter was caught up in the events of that chaotic year and became not only the chronicler of the most interesting killing ever in St. Augustine, but as "Shannon Smith," a character in her own story.

Nancy Powell as Bureau Chief for the *Florida Times-Union* moved easily in the circles that controlled the day-to-day happenings in a city suffering the hangover from an intrusive civil rights fight waged by the Rev. Martin Luther King, Jr. As a refined Southern lady, Powell was a St. Johns County insider, respected for her abilities, trusted for her deep Southern roots and socially sought after because of the power of her position with the most influential newspaper in North Florida.

Newspaper reporters and editors will forever debate the merits of becoming part of the story being pursued, and this book should be a case study in every Journalism school. Nancy Powell as the lead reporter became such a part of the unfolding events that she could not be assigned to the story at the time of the criminal trial and in fact was a witness for the prosecution. Further, the law profession should take a special interest in this work because many of the same elements of the celebrated O. J. Simpson trial were present in this case. The superb legal defense work could have been used as a blueprint by the Simpson lawyers.

Residents of St. Augustine and St. Johns County will find this book painful, for it portrays the community as it was and in many ways still is. St. Augustine is still a cliquish city and visitors and newcomers are welcome to

i

gawk at the façade of the tourist industry but not upset the internal workings of an efficient social order and political system. Many of the characters in this book have passed from the scene but their replacements are in plentiful supply and the events of 1974 are still possible today.

In reviving this long dormant manuscript, two old newspaper people found the story fresh with many new leads to follow. The writers of this story found it interesting that the division of opinions as to what really happened in that fateful year of 1974 remain. As the judge who heard the case in court put it ". . . There were those who believed he was innocent, those who believed he was guilty and those who believed she (the victim) deserved what she got."

This amazing story is an important part of the long history of St. Augustine and will long be debated and argued over. It is the hope of the authors of this book that the passing of time will release the keepers of the secrets of that bloody murder from their stoic silence. This book contains many answers. All that is needed to finally close this sordid event in St. Augustine's history is for the truth to be told by those who know it so well.

For Nancy Powell this book is a crowning achievement and a tribute to an outstanding career as a first-rate newspaper reporter.

As a writing team we apologize to grammarians everywhere. This incredible story is told in the newspaper style in which we are most comfortable.

---30---

Jim Mast--1998

Chapter 1

Year of the Tiger

The unseasonably warm day of January 23, 1974, was the beginning of the Chinese Year of the Tiger, and a year-long public nightmare in the coastal city of St. Augustine, Florida. An invisible historical aura draws thousands of tourists into the narrow downtown streets annually in blatant contrast to life in neighboring areas of St. Johns County which, at that time, were mostly rural.

The grisly murder, which took place at sunset in an old established bayfront residential area in downtown St. Augustine, was as unexpected as rape in a kindergarten. Police who investigated the slaying classified it as one of the most vicious attacks on an individual in the history of the more than four century old city. And, that's a lot of history.

That morning, sunshine, the hallmark of Florida, bathed every historical corner of the ancient city as tourists began making the sightseeing rounds. There wasn't a single foreboding cloud in the sky. Nor, was there so much as a faint whisper in the briny breeze that gently ruffled the blue-grey water around the fishing and pleasure craft adrift in Matanzas Bay, to hint of the impending tragedy that would raise goose flesh for months to come. It was Athalia Ponsell Lindsley, the murder victim herself, a 56-year-old former model and show girl, who set the stage for the tragedy as she had noon lunch at "Seafair," a popular seafood restaurant, located across the Bridge of Lions that connects the old city's downtown area with the island known as Davis Shores. Athalia sat at a round table by the window with her fourth husband, James Lindsley, a former St. Augustine mayor, and two guests.

It was perhaps providential that one of the guests was Shannon Smith, a reporter, who would, just hours later, write the first account of a murder police described as the most heinous slaying in St. Augustine in nearly a century. Shannon ran the St. Augustine news bureau for *The Florida Times-Union,* based in Jacksonville. The other guest was Albert Kay, a fellow real estate associate of former Mayor Lindsley. Shannon had written numerous stories in which one or the other of the Lindsleys was involved, but she was not lunching with them for business reasons that particular day. It was just a friendly get-together.

Shannon had known Athalia and Jim longer than they had known each other. She had met Athalia in Jacksonville in the 1950's, soon after she retired from her New York career as fashion model and part-time

Broadway show girl. She had met Jim two years before he met and married Athalia, still a tall, striking blonde with classic bone structure who, at 56, had maintained her good looks and a blade thin waistline. She moved with the same poised, swan like grace, which, at the peak of her career, had helped her to become one of John Robert Powers' highest paid models.

During the luncheon, Athalia dominated the conversation by talking about knives. Using a fork to cut into the fried fresh flounders on her plate, she warned her husband and guests not to use their knives.

"It's the Chinese New Year. Knives are bad luck today," she said with a touch of ingrained drama.

She went on to say that it was the first day of the Chinese Year of the Tiger, which comes around every 12 years. For her, The Year of the Tiger had a special meaning. Early on in her marriage to Lindsley, Jim had nicknamed her "Tigerina" because of the rather fierce determination with which she went about doing things. Athalia's companions were more amused than alarmed as she elaborated on Chinese superstition and fear of knives. They attributed the comments to her unusual interest in Chinese history and customs and to her tendency to overdramatize almost everything. After all, the stage had been her life for more than two decades. Thus, her warnings did not raise hackles until much later in the day.

During the meal, Athalia rambled on about the Oriental dinner she was planning to prepare that evening to celebrate the New Year. After lunch, Athalia and Jim would be heading up the road about 40 miles to Jacksonville, Athalia's former home, and still her favorite place to shop. It was in Jacksonville supermarkets that she expected to find snow peas, Chinese cabbage and other dinner ingredients not readily available in St. Augustine at that time. During the four months they had been married, the Lindsleys had scarcely missed a week of making the trip to Jacksonville for one reason or another.

The Lindsleys and their guests finished lunch about one o'clock and then rode in separate cars to a downtown parking lot adjacent to Lindsley's real estate office that was housed on the first floor of his childhood home--a more than 300-year-old coquina rock Spanish structure near the corner of St. George and King Streets, directly across the street from Trinity Parish, Florida's oldest Episcopal Church. Although the Lindsley home was listed on the National Register of Historic Structures, the old house was in sad need of repairs. For safety reasons, the second and third floors had been boarded up for several years. Rumor had it that the upper floors were haunted.

Shannon Smith rode into town with Athalia in the 1956 Cadillac Athalia referred to as her "black pearl" although there were rusted out holes in the floor board of the car and the seat springs were peeking through portions of the upholstery. It wasn't that Athalia couldn't afford to buy a new car. She didn't want one. She was convinced that since World War II, the automotive industry had been turning out junk. Lindsley and Albert Kay rode together in Jim's late model green Pinto station wagon that Lindsley insisted on driving when he and Athalia made out-of-town trips. Jim didn't win many arguments with his headstrong wife but he stood firm on that one issue. Reaching the parking lot, he dropped off Kay and waited with the motor running for Athalia to say her goodbyes to Shannon and park the Cadillac, dropping coins in the five-hour meter before joining him for the trip to Jacksonville.

Athalia had brought along a camel-colored wool coat which, because of the 80 degree temperatures, she did not need. She tossed the coat into the back of the station wagon, already cluttered with fishing gear, maps, boxes of ammunition for hunting guns, a bottle of Maalox, a carton of cigarettes and a machete Jim used to cut away underbrush when he was showing rural property to real estate clients. Athalia eyed the cigarettes with disapproval.

"Jimmy, darling, you smoke too much. It's going to kill you," she scolded.

"Hell . . . everybody's going to die of something," he snorted, reaching in his shirt pocket for another Winston. The Lindsleys were not seen again in St. Augustine until about five thirty that afternoon when Jim parked the Pinto outside the St. Augustine Post office and waited for Athalia to go inside and mail letters she had been carrying around in her purse all day.

When Athalia returned to the car, Lindsley drove her directly to the parking lot where she had left the old Cadillac. There, they separated their purchases, transferring two large bags of groceries into Athalia's car and leaving the bag that contained the ingredients for the Chinese dinner in the station wagon.

Then, after a brief discussion about their plans for the evening, Athalia kissed her husband, got behind the wheel of the car, and drove off alone in the direction of her home on South Marine Street. Jim walked next door to his office to check for messages on the telephone answering machine before driving across the historic Bridge of Lions to a house on Lew Boulevard near St.

Augustine Beach. The knowledge that he maintained the residence separately from Athalia triggered rumors in the community that the marriage was in trouble.

Athalia and Jim had agreed that Athalia would meet him at his home to begin dinner preparations after she put away her purchases and fed her menagerie of pets that included dogs, goats and a crippled bluejay.

As was her custom, she approached her Marine Street home from the rear driveway off Charlotte Street, one of St. Augustine's many narrow, one-way streets. She chanced being spotted by a police officer and drove the wrong way on Charlotte to save herself about four blocks of driving. It really wasn't much of a risk because prowl cars didn't spend much time in that neighborhood. A waitress, Joy Claire, who lived on Charlotte Street in a house that faced Athalia's back entrance, looked out the window and spotted the black Cadillac moving down the one-way-street in the wrong direction and called to her husband: "Here comes Mrs. Lindsley, driving the wrong way again."

As Athalia approached the back entrance, the neighborhood was quiet except for a thin volley of laughter drifting from the national cemetery, a block north of her home. Children were engaging in a favorite pastime and were playing hide and seek among tombstones that marked the graves of 180 men who were massacred by the Seminole Indians back in 1863. Neighbors, who had been working in their yards when Athalia left home earlier in the day, had disappeared.

Athalia parked in the area just outside the locked gate of the chain-link fence that enclosed her back yard. After unlocking the gate and the back door to the house, she carried in the groceries and set them along with her purse on the kitchen floor, leaving her keys dangling in the lock of the back door.

A few minutes before six o'clock, Charlotte Cooper, a woman who lived in an apartment house on the east side of Marine Street, across from Athalia's big white house, looked out of an upstairs window and saw Athalia crossing the front lawn, trailed by a hobbling bluejay. Athalia had rescued the bird from a cat a few months earlier. Because it had suffered a broken wing, she had been keeping it in a contrived cardboard cage on a table by the front door, waiting for its wing to mend. At least once a day she took the bird outdoors for exercise. Ms. Cooper had watched Athalia walk to the edge of the yard and pick up the afternoon newspaper. As Athalia turned back toward the house, her neighbor left the window and went to another room to turn on the television. It was almost time for the six o'clock news. Athalia had only minutes to live.

Another pair of eyes, glazed with anger, watched as she carried the paper back to the porch where she frequently sat on the steps in the late afternoon, reading the paper or her mail while the crippled bird instinctively poked for insects in the thick mat of lawn grass. Shortly after Athalia reached the porch, the angry-eyed observer emerged from his hiding place, waving a formidable thick-bladed weapon, and began chopping her to death.

The assailant struck and cut her many times, slicing off a finger on her right hand and nearly taking off her head with one of the blows. The killer left her sprawled on the front walkway in a pool of blood, her head barely attached to her body by threads of crimson flesh.

Athalia took her last moaning breath as a setting sun glowed like a giant blood orange over the bay across from her home. The eyes on her detached head were open wide, but they could not comprehend the spectacularly beautiful scene. The Spanish, who settled St. Augustine, had named the bay Matanzas--a word that, roughly translated, means bloody massacre.

Chapter 2

Eyewitness to Murder

No strangers to murder, St. Augustine police were as shaken as anyone else by the brazen slaughter of Athalia Lindsley and reached the swift conclusion that the killer had acted in a blind rage, oblivious to the possibility he might be seen.

Certainly, the odds were poor that there would be no eyewitnesses to an attack executed in broad daylight on a doorstep fronting a street that served as the main artery to the only hospital in town. The dark shadows of evening had not yet fallen. Earlier in the month the state of Florida had shifted to Daylight Saving Time, ninety days ahead of schedule, as an experiment in energy conservation. Because of the unusually warm January weather, windows of neighboring homes were open, increasing chances that someone would hear the victim if she screamed or called for help.

At six o'clock, Rosemary McCormick, a middle-aged woman who lived in a slate colored shingled house on the north side of Athalia's Marine Street home, and Rosemary's mother, Lucille Smith, were in the kitchen of the McCormick home. Rosemary's husband, Connie, was away on a hunting trip in Mexico. Their nineteen-year-old son, Locke, was in the den, reading a tennis magazine, waiting for his mother and grandmother to put supper on the table.

Lucille, recently widowed, lived in a red brick bungalow on the east side of Marine Street, directly across from the walkway where the murder took place. The morning of the day of the murder, Rosemary had invited Lucille to join her and Locke for dinner that evening. About 10 minutes before six, Lucille had walked over to her daughter's home. As she left her house, Lucille had noticed Athalia in the corner of her front yard and was surprised to see her wearing street clothes instead of the old pink robe Lucille had frequently observed her wearing while digging in the yard. Lucille did not approve of women gardening in their night clothes. In fact, there was little if anything about Athalia of which Lucille approved. Such a strange, disagreeable woman, Lucille thought, as she crossed the street without bothering to speak, pretending she did not see her. Athalia, in turn, had ignored Lucille.

Ten minutes or so later, Rosemary was in the process of removing a roast from the oven and Lucille was setting the table for dinner when the two women heard unusual noises coming from outside.

"What on earth is that?" Rosemary asked.

"Beats me," Lucille replied, not immediately alarmed. In the den, Locke was distracted from his reading by the same sounds. Because the den was closer than the kitchen to the source of the noise, the sounds were clearer but none the less puzzling. Throwing down his magazine, Locke ran to an open casement window that faced the north side of Athalia's home. At the window, he could hear moaning and a brisker sound like the clapping of hands.

Unable to see anyone from the window, Locke ran to the front door and out into the yard. Looking across to Athalia's yard, he saw the back of a man with greyish hair who was leaning over something or someone on the front walkway of the house. The man's right shoulder was moving in a downward, swinging motion like he was chopping wood. The moaning Locke thought he had heard had stopped and as he ran across the yard to get a better view of what was happening, the clapping noise also ceased. The man who had been swinging at something on the ground was standing straight but his back was still turned and Locke could not see his face as the assailant slowly walked away, disappearing around the south corner of Athalia's house.

As the man moved away, Locke had his first glimpse of the massacred body sprawled on the walkway like a victim in an Alfred Hitchcock thriller. For a moment, Locke stood frozen in horror, not quite believing the macabre sight. Then, like a scalded dog, he raced back to the house to call the police, brushing by his mother and grandmother, who had come from the kitchen, looking for him. The city police dispatcher logged Locke's call at 6:07 p.m. Shortly before an ambulance and two police cars with screaming sirens barreled down the street in response to the call, a man drove South on Marine Street in a white Volkswagen. The driver passed Athalia's house and slowed his speed as the car reached a house where B.O. Brunson, an elderly resident, was sitting in a rocker on the front porch. As the car snailed by, the driver leaned out the window and yelled to Brunson: "Somebody call an ambulance. A woman up the street just fell out of a window and there's blood everywhere."

Brunson was on his way inside to the telephone when he heard a siren, turned around and saw an ambulance streak by. From his front yard, Brunson watched as the ambulance screeched to a halt at the edge of the big white house four doors north on the other side of the street. A few minutes later, he saw the first two of a battery of police cars, with flashing blue lights and screaming sirens, pull up behind the ambulance.

From where he was standing, Brunson couldn't see the walkway where Athalia lay. Although only the portion of Athalia's yard nearest the street was visible, he did not go to the scene until after doors of houses all around him began banging, and neighbors, alarmed by the multiple sirens, emerged from their houses like school children in a fire drill. Brunson was still at home when a pretty dark-haired woman he recognized as the wife of Alan G. Stanford, the manager of St. Johns County, came flying out of the Spanish-type stuccoed house on the south side of the Lindsley home. She met Rosemary McCormick at the curb near the ambulance. Rosemary had gone outside immediately after Locke had raced by her, yelling, in a near state of hysteria. She had never seen her son so upset. After taking one brief look at the bloody spectacle on the walkway in the yard next-door, Rosemary had run across the grass, yelling, "Alan . . . Alan."

Although Alan had not responded, Rosemary had continued walking toward the Stanford home, and as she reached the edge of the yard, she saw Alan Stanford's wife, Patti, approaching the arched gateway in the cement wall surrounding the Stanfords' front yard. After closing the gate, Patti stood blocking the entrance, and catching her breath that came in gasps when she spoke. Her face was pale as a bed sheet and her eyes were wild with excitement or fear. Rosemary was not sure which.

The two women had disappeared when Brunson finally walked up the street and joined the carnival-like crowd that had begun to gather in morbid curiosity on the lawn near Athalia's mutilated body.

Never in his 68 years had Brunson witnessed a more horrific sight. The victim's hair, her face . . . every inch of the dead woman was covered with blood. Athalia's blue flowered silk dress was pulled up around her waist, clinging to her body in crimson shreds. The lower portion of her body was nude. Her eyes were open wide in a blank stare.

A woman, whom Brunson had never seen before, was running out of the yard as he approached and had tried to warn him. "It's like something out of a horror movie. Her head--it's almost cut off. I wish I hadn't looked."

It was just as the driver who yelled at Brunson had said. Blood had splattered everywhere--on the grass, the walkway, the porch steps and even the white walls near the entrance of the house. Brunson also noticed a green hose dripping water in the grass. Someone had apparently tried to wash away some of the blood but there was still so much left it made him ill. A string of pearls, broken during the attack, and one blue kid pump lay in a wet patch of blood near the victim.

Athalia was still wearing the mate to the shoe.

As Brunson moved across the yard, he heard a voice in the gathering saying: "Nobody liked her much, but this is monstrous."

A dapper looking white haired man had responded. "She was a terrible woman."

Then, Brunson spotted one of his neighbors, Oliver Lawton, clerk of the St. Johns County Circuit Court, quietly leading his wife away from the scene. His wife, in turn, was pulling at the leash of a Persian cat she had intended to take for a walk.

A young looking, grey-haired man Brunson didn't recognize was talking to a city police officer in an angry voice. "You've got to get these people out of here--rope off the yard. Where the hell is the sheriff?"

Brunson didn't stay around to hear the answer. He had a bad heart and pains had started shooting across his chest and down his left arm. Although he had intended to speak to the police about the man in the white car, he simply wasn't up to hanging around.

It was not until the following day when investigators went through the Marine Street neighborhood looking for possible eye witnesses to the murder that he told the police about the driver of the white car who had yelled to him the previous evening. "He was young--Oriental looking with bushy-hair; wearing either a long-sleeved white shirt or jacket. Maybe it was a white uniform." Brunson really couldn't be sure.

He told the police that about five minutes or so before the car drove by he thought he had heard screams coming from somewhere up the street, north of his house.

From his porch, he could not see the walkway where Athalia Lindsley was being slashed to death. So, he had attributed the screaming to the children he had seen earlier, playing in the National Cemetery.

"Kids play hide and seek there a lot and they get pretty loud sometimes," Brunson said, adding that he had not moved from his rocking chair until the man in the white car drove by. No, he said, he didn't recall seeing anyone else on the street before the ambulance arrived. One of his neighbors, Mrs. Frances Bemis, was in the habit of taking a walk around six every evening and she usually called to him if he was sitting on the porch when she passed the house. If she or anyone else had walked by that evening, he hadn't noticed.

Brunson said he had been "sort of" glancing through the evening newspaper and he might not even have noticed the white car if the "bushy haired guy who was driving" hadn't yelled.

Years later, the identity of the driver remains one of the puzzling aspects in the case. Interest in trying to find him waned when Brunson died of a heart attack a few weeks later.

Chapter 3

Reporting the News

The morning after the murder, Shannon Smith's telephone rang at 6 o'clock. The caller was James Lindsley and he was spitting mad.

The object of his anger was the story about Athalia's murder the *Florida Times-Union* had run front page that morning along with a photograph of the victim, resurrected from the newspaper's photo library.

Shannon knew Jim was clutching the paper because she could hear it crackle when he paused to light a cigarette and then, as often happened when he was really teed off, he began coughing and choking on the smoke.

What had upset him was a single paragraph about halfway down in the story that said "Lindsley learned of his wife's death when located by police at the home of City Attorney Robert Andreu."

"That part about the police finding me at Robbie's is a damn lie. It sounds terrible. I demand a retraction," Lindsley stormed. His voice was so loud that the vibrations awakened the long-haired black cat, curled on the bed beside Shannon.

The reporter made a feeble attempt at humor to try and calm Jim. "You are upsetting 'Albert'," she said.

"I don't give a damn about that cat. I want to know what you are going to do about correcting this lie," Jim continued to rant.

Most of the problem stemmed from Shannon's not learning about the murder until more than an hour after it happened. In the haste of putting together a story in time to meet the paper's nine o'clock evening deadline, she had been forced to go mostly with the scanty information the police were cautiously giving out. She told Jim she had tried to reach him off and on for nearly two hours and when she had called Chief of Police Virgil Stuart at his home around 7:30, he told her the police also had been unsuccessful in locating Jim. Unfortunately, Stuart was still at home eating dinner and had not yet gone to the murder scene. Everything he could tell Shannon was secondhand information.

At that time Shannon was on good terms with Athalia's neighbor, County Manager Stanford and his wife, Patti. Hoping he might have seen Jim Lindsley or know something the police were not reporting about the murder, Shannon had called Stanford around 8:30 p.m.

His daughter, Patricia, answered and said her father was outside, talking to the police. She would get him. When Stanford came to the phone, he sounded annoyed and was of no help. To Shannon's dismay, he said only that he had been sleeping when the phone rang and did not appreciate being disturbed. Apparently Patricia had been mistaken when she said he was outside, or he was lying for reasons Shannon could not understand. It gave the reporter her first cause to wonder if he might be guilty of murdering Athalia.

Much later in the evening, when she had an opportunity to discuss her call to Stanford with Sheriff Dudley Garrett, he confirmed that Stanford had not been asleep at 8:30.

Minutes before Shannon's deadline for filing a story, Chief Stuart called to tell her the police finally had located Lindsley. Stuart said Jim was with Robbie Andreu, the city attorney. Shannon was never sure how the words "home of" got into the sentence in the newspaper story. It was one of those unfortunate errors that sometimes occur when a story has to be dictated under pressure by telephone to a rewrite editor. Shannon's mental state that evening had not helped anything. She had put together what facts she could muster in a state of semi-shock over Athalia's murder.

She apologized to Jim.

"I guess I misunderstood Chief Stuart. I'm going to write a follow-up story today and I promise I'll clear it up. Just tell me what you would like me to say."

Sounding calmer but still grim, Jim said it wasn't something he wanted to discuss over the phone and more or less demanded that she meet him at "Seafair" for lunch. "I don't know if I can eat a bite of anything but I want this thing cleared up TODAY," he said.

Shannon hesitated and then as she started to respond, Jim interrupted in another burst of anger.

"What's wrong? Are you afraid of me? You think I killed her? I loved her. You of all people should know that."

Shannon already had an early morning press conference in Chief Stuart's office and another appointment scheduled with Sheriff Dudley Garrett at noon. But, she agreed to meet Lindsley at 10:30 that morning at McCartney's, a drug store with a lunch and soda fountain around the corner from Lindsley's office. Lindsley arrived first and ordered a cup of tea. He hoped the tea would soothe his ulcers that had been aggravated by the large amount of coffee he had consumed during the night, as he sat alone in his living room, trying to come to terms with what had happened. Jim's face was grey as an overcast sky next to the white windbreaker he was wearing pulled up around his neck. He seemed to be having a chill. His hazel eyes mirrored a mixture of shock and anger. When Shannon arrived, he had just taken a white pill from a bottle in his jacket pocket. She watched him lay it on his tongue and wash it down with a large gulp of hot tea.

"My ulcer medicine," he explained, blotting his lips with a paper napkin. In recent years, he had undergone three rounds of surgery for ulcers and cancer. There had been a time he would have eased his pain with a shot or two of bourbon. Athalia had been instrumental in getting him to swear off booze. Her motives were not strictly for health reasons. She was aware there were people in St. Augustine who still blamed Jim's overindulgence in alcohol for the death of his first wife, Lillian. Jim had been at the wheel that New Year's Eve in 1971 when Lillian was killed in a two-car collision at a Highway U. S. 1 intersection. The Lindsley car had moved forward on a green light and was struck when a second driver, emerging from a side road, ignored the red light and shot into the path of the Lindsley vehicle. The collision resulted in Lillian's neck being broken and in Jim escaping with a fractured skull. The Florida Highway Patrol did not charge him in the accident but because of his reputation as a heavy drinker, there still were people who blamed him for Lillian's death.

Lindsley was haunted anew by the accusations the morning after Athalia's terrible death. Before Shannon arrived, he decided to tell her about Lillian's death before she heard it secondhand. He launched right into the story, explaining that the gossip about Lillian's death was one of the reasons he was so upset over Shannon's story, reporting that he had gone to the home of his longtime friend and attorney the previous evening. "Between you and me, I feel like a jinx . . . with one wife dead from a broken neck and another with her head chopped off," he said.

He also told Shannon that the older of his two sons from his first marriage had been decapitated in a motorcycle accident.

Shannon smiled at Jim's ironic choice of words because "Jinx" was Jim Lindsley's nickname. "Now," Shannon said, thankful for the moment of levity, "Tell me about last night. I really tried to call you at home several times. I couldn't get an answer. Honest."

"I hope you're not in a hurry," Jim said. "It is important to me that the story gets told right." Without waiting for an answer, Jim began relating the events of the previous day, saying he had kissed Athalia goodbye at the downtown parking lot about 5:30 and watched her drive away to her rendezvous with death. He had stopped by his office and then headed home, stopping en route at a convenience market to buy coffee cream. It was there he ran into Frank and Hamilton Upchurch, two prominent St. Augustine attorneys. A few minutes before six he drove into the driveway of his Lew Boulevard residence. He had looked at his watch because he didn't want to miss the six o'clock news on television. He stayed outside just long enough to turn on the lawn sprinklers and walk to the edge of the yard, looking for the afternoon newspaper. One of his neighbors, who was outside, told him the delivery of the paper was going to be late because the presses at the *St. Augustine Record* had broken down earlier that afternoon.

"I was really steamed," he said. "I wanted to see if there had been anything written in the paper about Athalia's visit to the county commission meeting Tuesday afternoon." Disappointed, Lindsley said he went inside to call his wife.

"I wanted to ask her if her paper had been delivered and, if it had, to bring it along when she came to prepare our dinner. I let the phone ring 15 or 20 times-- maybe more--to give Athalia time to answer in case she was in the yard."

Jim said Athalia was in the habit of taking the bluejay outside for a constitutional in the early evening and she often sat on the front steps, reading her mail while the bird hopped around. "She tried to keep an eye on the bird because of neighborhood cats," he said.

Failing to get an answer, Jim had hung up, turned on the television, watched the news for 10 minutes before dialing Athalia's number again. "I guess she was already dead by that time," he sighed. "When she didn't answer, I thought she must be on her way over. I went back to watching the news and it was winding up when the telephone rang. It was Esther Stookey, a friend of Athalia's."

Esther lived nearby in an apartment on St. George Street. When Athalia's mother was alive, Esther had frequently sat with the elderly invalid when Athalia was away from the house.

"Stookey told me something terrible had happened on Marine Street . . . there were police all over the place and I should get myself down there. I was getting into the car when the phone rang again." Jean Troemel, a local artist and friend, was calling to tell him something bad had happened to his wife.

"I asked her 'what'? She said 'the worst'"

Jean had been purposely stingy with her information, saying only that she had passed Athalia's house on her way to an art association meeting and had stopped when she saw police cars and an ambulance. After talking to the police, she had returned home to call Jim.

"I guess I exceeded all the speed limits to get down there, but I wasn't stopped, probably because most of the police force was already down at Athalia's. It really scorched me that Virgil or someone else had not called," Jim fumed.

He said his old friend, Robbie Andreu, was standing in the yard talking to County Commissioner Dick Parks when Lindsley reached his wife's house. Dick, who lived in the restored area of the old walled city, a few blocks from Athalia's home, had heard about the murder on the radio and had walked down there. "Robbie also had heard the radio report and had gone down there, expecting to find me."

Two of the police officers at the scene had immediately asked Jim to go with them through the house to determine if anything had been stolen.

"Robbie offered to go with me so I guess that is how the story got started that police found me with the city attorney," Lindsley said, pausing to wave to the waitress to bring fresh tea. His voice had grown husky from talking and chain-smoking. He thought the tea would help. Continuing, he described Athalia's house as a "real mess."

He said police officers had tracked in a lot of blood on the floors and carpets. As best I could tell, nothing was missing except Clementine . . . that jay with the broken wing. The cage Athalia had rigged for the bird looked like it had been struck by something. One side had a big dent. He said all of Athalia's jewelry, except a jade necklace she had left for repair in Jacksonville that day and the pearls she had been wearing at the time of death, was in the usual place in a box on a dresser in the upstairs bedroom. Athalia's purse was on the floor in the kitchen. Jim said he examined the contents and found quite a large amount of cash in a billfold. He also had mentally inventoried paintings, silver and antiques.

"I'm satisfied the son of a bitch who killed her didn't go there to commit robbery," Jim added, his face flushing in anger.

During the conversation, Lindsley said he understood Sheriff Dudley Garrett was taking over the investigation. "He's a good man. I sure hope he can nail the maniac who cut her up."

Lindsley didn't mention that one of his close friends, Joe McClure, who owned the company that operated trailer trains for tourists in St. Augustine, had come to his home after his return from viewing Athalia's butchered body. It was McClure who told Shannon Smith he had driven to Lindsley's house after hearing news of the murder on the radio.

When Jim opened the door, I asked him right away "did you kill Athalia?"

McClure said Lindsley's face turned purple with anger and he grabbed a shotgun he kept by the front door and pointed it at his old friend.

"You son of a bitch. How can you ask such a question? I ought to let you have it," he fumed.

At the press conference held in Police Chief Virgil Stuart's office the morning after the murder, Stuart said robbery had been ruled out as a possible motive for the murder. "It was hate--pure hate. Somebody hated her guts. As for suspects, everyone is a suspect except maybe that little lady over there," the chief added, pointing to Shannon Smith.

"She doesn't have the strength to deliver the kind of blows that contributed to the death of Mrs. Lindsley."

Police were still searching for the murder weapon and Stuart was of the opinion that the assailant "had to have used a meat cleaver or a thick bladed bush knife such as a machete." He said the only clue to the killer's identity was a description supplied by the neighbor boy, Locke McCormick, who had watched as a man in a white shirt and dark trousers walked away from the scene.

Stuart ignored a reporter who commented that "apparently the killer was in no rush to get away."

The chief said Locke had described the killer as "kind of middle-sized, under six feet, on the thin side with grey hair."

Police officers who responded to Locke's call found a trail of blood droplets that led from the body to a three-foot concrete wall and hedge that separated the Lindsley home from County Manager Alan Stanford's property. The trail of blood ended in the grass about halfway around the house.

A *St. Augustine Record* reporter, Patrick Lynn, leaped on that bit of information like a starving mountain lion. "Does this mean Alan Stanford is a suspect?" Lynn asked.

"Now, hold on there Patrick, I didn't say that," the chief scowled.

Chief Stuart had managed to circumvent several other of Lynn's questions, including one concerning a rumor that Athalia was not wearing underpants when her body was found. "We are pretty sure she wasn't raped. I believe the autopsy will confirm that," Stuart said. The chief believed Mrs. Lindsley had been attacked outdoors, perhaps while she was reaching for the mail in the box by the front door. The police had found several unopened letters, saturated in the blood, under her body.

Stuart ended the press conference, declaring the slaying of Athalia Lindsley to be the most vicious of any murder that had occurred in St. Augustine during his 40 years with the police department. He also asked reporters not to use the name of the young neighbor who had run outside during the attack and watched the murderer walk away. "His mother fears for his life," Stuart explained.

Most of the reporters had agreed but Locke's name was used by every newspaper and every radio and television station in the area after the *St. Augustine Record* chose to ignore the request and identified the eyewitness in a front page story that appeared a few hours after the press conference.

Chapter 4

An Incredible Life

Athalia Ponsell Lindsley had gravitated to the limelight most of her life. Right or wrong, one way or another, she had commanded attention, returning to center stage, again and again, until finally in death, she had stolen the show in St. Augustine, Florida, the oldest stage in the country.

Because of her remembered successes in New York City as model, actress, dancer, and as talk show hostess on Bud Collyier's "Winner Take All" show in the early days of television, national wire services carried the gory details of her murder and, in the aftermath of the tragedy, reporters from all over Florida flocked like vultures to St. Augustine.

Athalia Lindsley's personality was like a shattered mosaic with so many parts that no one, including four husbands, ever succeeded in piecing together the whole picture. As they say, she marched to a different drummer, a beat only she could hear; loving and hating with incredible dimension; never lukewarm about any of her relationships. When it suited her purposes, she was capable of great compassion but she could also be spitefully judgmental. She had such strong opinions and such an acute sense of right and wrong that she stood ready to defend her principals with a tongue as sharp as the machete that ended her life.

In St. Augustine, where she had lived barely two years before she was hacked to death, her critics outnumbered her admirers. As early as the night of her terrible death, some of those critics already were saying, "she deserved what she got."

She had been born rich as well as beautiful, the daughter of Margaret and Charles Fetter, natives of Ohio. Her father was a utilities magnate who built a marble mansion on the Isle of Pines, just south of Cuba, where the family lived for almost a decade before moving to Jacksonville when Athalia was 12 years old.

In her new environment, Athalia became a model student, scholastically outshining many of her schoolmates, first at a parochial school in St. Augustine, where their parents sent Athalia and her younger sister, Geraldine for a brief period, and later at Robert E. Lee High School in Jacksonville. At the latter school she captured the limelight by starring in school plays; winning beauty pageants and essay contests; playing piano at school talent nights; excelling at almost everything she undertook.

Seemingly, she had everything going for her. After graduating from Lee High, she enrolled at the University of Mexico at Mexico City where she mastered Spanish, French, and German. Yet, the problems encountered in many of her relationships indicated she never really learned the art of communications in any language.

Athalia's studies in Mexico were interrupted by the death of her father. She went home to attend the funeral and never returned to school. Instead, she decided to head for New York on a lark and ended up staying for two decades. Her classic bone structure enabled her easily to become one of John Robert Powers' highest paid models. But, success as a model wasn't enough to satisfy her frenetic drives.

Between modeling assignments, she began dancing with Broadway chorus lines and picked up bit parts in two Hollywood movies.

She always attracted glamorous men and at one time her list of suitors included such illustrious personalities as actor Tyrone Power and Joseph Kennedy Jr., the brother of President John Kennedy, and political heir-apparent. He was killed while on active duty in World War II and his potentials and ambitions were permanently thwarted. Newspapers had carried pictures of Athalia visiting in Palm Beach with the Kennedy family where Joseph Jr. allegedly presented her with a French poodle and a diamond ring before he was cut down in the war. She had photos of herself with Kennedy and the dog in an album that was prominently displayed on a library table in the foyer of her Marine Street home. Modesty was not one of her virtues. When she spoke of her old beau, Joe Kennedy, a kind of reverence crept into her voice. Although she had become a political conservative, a registered Republican, and a member of the John Birch Society, she refused ever to brook a word of criticism about the Kennedy family or their political views. That family was perhaps her only sacred cow for she was often ruthless in her judgment of politicians.

After Joe Kennedy was killed, many other suitors waited in the wings to court Athalia. Three of the romances that followed resulted in brief and stormy marriages. Although she obviously thrived on the attention men paid her, something in her personality prevented her from enjoying an enduring connubial relationship.

When Athalia gave up her modeling career in 1955 and returned to Jacksonville, she was pretty much soured on men. She plunged into new projects; writing a book on gardening, patenting an electric device for scouring pots and studying for and passing an exam that licensed her as a Florida real estate agent. None of her activities stopped her from meddling in Jacksonville politics. She became embroiled in so many local controversies that by 1969, people were calling her the "Watch Dog" of City Hall. But, councilmen listened to her rantings and did as they pleased, so in 1970 she decided to abandon the local scene and run as a Republican candidate for a seat in the Florida State Legislature. When she lost the election, a Jacksonville political writer, attributed her defeat to her "ultra conservative" views. Athalia took the comment as a compliment.

She might have made a political comeback if her mother had not suffered a fall that fractured her hip and collar bone and turned her into an invalid. Athalia was devoted to her mother and refused to shunt her off to a nursing home.

For a period of time between 1971 and her mother's death in April of 1973, Athalia vanished from the public eye to give Margaret Fetter the best possible home care. While her mother rested in a rented hospital-type bed set up in the downstairs of the big family home on Riverside Avenue in Jacksonville, Athalia administered to her needs and for many weeks slept on a pallet on the floor, awakening at the slightest movement or sound coming from her mother's bed. She massaged her mother's massive bruises, shifted her to different positions to guard against bed sores and prepared special meals which she hoped would help her mother to regain her strength. Mrs. Fetter responded to the care but the surgery on her hip was unsuccessful, permanently confining her to a wheel chair.

The big, 10-room family home eventually became too much for Athalia to maintain without servants. With some difficulty, she talked her mother into selling the house to an insurance company in need of the land for expansion purposes. After some rather shrewd negotiations on the part of Athalia, the company agreed to purchase the property for $100,000, an offer her mother could not refuse.

Since leaving St. Joseph's Academy in St. Augustine, Athalia had carried a torch for the ancient Spanish city. In her opinion, it was cleaner, prettier and, in a political sense more peaceful than Jacksonville. In April of 1972, Athalia bought the big pseudo-Spanish house at 124 Marine Street in St. Augustine and moved in with her mother, five dogs, two goats and all of the family antiques and heirlooms, kidding herself that she had found paradise.

She erred in believing life in St. Augustine would be more serene than her life in Jacksonville. A victim of her own eccentricities, she would never enjoy any degree of peace.

Athalia continued to devote most of her energy to the care of her mother, leaving her side only long enough to shop for their needs and work in the yard. She loved planting seeds and shrubs and watching them sprout and grow. She mothered them like the children she never had. In the process of nursing her mother, she wasted away to 90 pounds and seemingly lost touch with the outside world with one or two exceptions. Shortly before her mother died, she invited 30 people to the Marine Street residence for a champagne luncheon, honoring the noted novelist, Taylor Caldwell. At the time, Mrs. Caldwell was living at Jacksonville Beach. Athalia had met her years before when the author addressed the Jacksonville Chapter of Penwomen International. When Athalia read in the newspaper that Mrs. Caldwell had moved into the Jacksonville area, Athalia burst from her self-imposed prison and began making elaborate plans to host her first big social event in many months.

The possibility that Taylor Caldwell would refuse an invitation from someone she barely knew never entered Athalia's mind. And, as it happened, the author did not refuse.

Athalia hired a waitress who lived in the neighborhood to help prepare and serve what the waitress described as "a ton of food." Athalia banked the living room and den area, where she had set up card tables for the guests to eat, with arrangements of fresh flowers, some of which she created with blossoms cut from her garden. Others were ordered from a local florist and rearranged by the ever-critical Athalia.

Incredibly, she found enough china, crystal stemware and silver in boxes that had not been unpacked since her move from Jacksonville to complete the 30 place settings. Most of the tableware belonged to Mrs. Fetter who had given large, elaborate parties during the years the family lived on the Isle of Pines.

Most of the guests invited to the luncheon for Taylor Caldwell were from Jacksonville because Athalia had made few friends in St. Augustine. That was partly because she had isolated herself to care for her mother, and her few contacts with local residents had been in the neighborhood and not of a pleasant nature. The few St. Augustine residents included Shannon Smith, who had met Athalia when both lived in Jacksonville, and Athalia's neighbor on South Street, Jean Troemel. None of the other neighbors were invited.

Almost from the day she moved into the Marine Street house, Athalia became embroiled in arguments with her next door neighbors, the McCormicks and the Stanfords. The disagreements began when Patti Stanford complained that the barking of the dogs Athalia locked in the garage at night was keeping Annette, the Stanfords' youngest daughter, from falling asleep at night. Annette was just a year old at the time. Mrs. Stanford was over 40 when Annette was born and the truth of the matter was she needed her rest as much or more than the child needed the sleep.

Athalia had never had children and was not especially sympathetic. In her mind, Patti Stanford's complaints were not justified. The dogs were not bothering Athalia's mother and she was a restless sleeper, easily awakened.

Soon after Mrs. Stanford complained, Rosemary McCormick also spoke to Athalia about the dogs. They were creating a nuisance in an otherwise peaceful neighborhood and Mrs. McCormick urged Athalia to "do something." She did nothing. To try and resolve the problem, Rosemary and her husband joined Mrs. Stanford in filing suit over the nuisance. Following the hearing on the suit, City Judge Richard Weinberg ordered Athalia to pay a $50 fine and to remove at least two of the dogs from the premises of her home. Athalia paid the fine and obeyed the order by boarding two of the dogs at a local kennel, but she was bitter. She truly missed the dogs and boarding them cost her $200 a month. So, the feuding with her neighbors continued.

Athalia and Patti's husband had begun squabbling after she installed a 10-foot high chain link fence around her yard and planted a thick bamboo hedge near the back driveway. Athalia's reason for installing the fence was to keep the dogs off the streets and prowlers out of her yard. But, Robert Frost's poetic contention that "good fences make good neighbors" didn't apply in the case of Athalia and Alan Stanford. The county manager viewed the chain-link structure as an eyesore and most of the neighbors agreed. Stanford began referring to it as the "spite fence" and he felt much the same about the bamboo hedge.

Whatever Stanford thought about the barricades, the fact was that his obstinate neighbor was terrified of break-ins. In addition to the high fence and locked gates, there were other signs--both inside and outside Athalia's house--of her need to protect herself. There was the "Beware Bad Dogs" sign posted near the gate to the back yard and the nearby giant floodlight that burned throughout the night. There was the loaded shot gun Athalia had placed at the corner of the front door and the pistol on her bedside table. The front and back entrance doors had double bolts and chains. There were telephones all over the house with the number for reaching police printed in red ink on stickers on the base of each instrument. Two phones, one green and one red, each with a different number, stood side by side on a table in the foyer. The green phone was Mrs. Fetter's private line but Athalia had elected not to have it disconnected after her mother's death in April of 1973. At the time, she had said she felt safer with two separate lines in the event of an emergency.

After her mother's funeral, Athalia put up a for-sale sign in the front yard, an indication she was contemplating moving from the neighborhood. Meantime, she decided to renew her real estate license and in the process, she met James Lindsley, who was then serving his second term as mayor of St. Augustine. There followed a whirlwind courtship that diverted Athalia and kept her away from home so much, she had very little time to fuss with the neighbors. The dust settled temporarily but it wouldn't stay that way. Athalia would see to it.

She became Mrs. James Lindsley on Sept. 23, 1973, in a quiet ceremony at Flagler Memorial Presbyterian Church. Athalia was a "cradle" Episcopalian and would have preferred an Anglican service but she had stubbornly refused to comply with a new canon rule that required couples getting married in the Episcopal Church to be counseled by a priest. She had gone to an acting priest at Trinity Episcopal Church, demanding that the requirement be waived but her request was denied.

Following the wedding and a brief honeymoon in South Florida, the newlyweds talked it over and decided to continue living in separate residences. Friends were told it was a temporary arrangement until Athalia could sell her house and decide what to do with the family collection of paintings and antiques. Riddled by fears of theft, she apparently was more concerned about her treasures than about the questions being raised about the state of her marriage. Even the couples' closest friends were beginning to wonder what might be wrong when four months after the ceremony, Athalia continued to sleep alone at night in the big house on Marine Street. More than once her husband, Jim, had joked publicly that his wife was staying on in her Marine Street house, partly to guard her treasures and partly to annoy her neighbor, Alan Stanford.

Sure enough, in October before she was killed, Athalia began a one-woman effort to get Stanford removed from his prestigious position. She was considering running for the county commission the following year if it took that kind of effort to get him out. She went on a witch hunt, digging into county records in the courthouse, and driving around the county, looking for roads in need of repair, drainage ditches that were not working properly, or anything for which Stanford, as county manager, might be blamed.

She also began regularly attending county commission meetings and would jump to her feet, in one histrionic outburst after another, to point a finger at Stanford, accusing him of everything imaginable from stealing pipe from the county road department to threatening to kill her. She also filed a complaint about the threat on her life with Sheriff Dudley Garrett.

Her final appearance before the county commission came the day before she was killed.

Chapter 5

Sheriff Garrett Takes Over

No one knows how or when the expression "if you want to commit murder, do it in St. Johns County" originated but it had been around a long time when Dudley Garrett Jr. exercised his authority as high sheriff of the county and took over the investigation of the Athalia Lindsley murder.

Florida Gov. Claude Kirk appointed Garrett sheriff in 1971 after Kirk removed longtime Sheriff L.O., Davis from office for malfeasance in office. "L.O.", as he was known to almost everyone in St. Johns County, was a lovable rascal and above all he was one of them. He gathered turtle eggs on the beach with them, threw a cast net for mullet, and generally enjoyed the same pastimes. No doubt he enjoyed many a gopher stew and turtle egg pound cake with the friendly natives. Because of his popularity, it was easy to turn a blind eye to his shortcomings. Many people thought his removal from office was political revenge by a Republican governor, because the malfeasance Sheriff Davis was charged with was a way of life in the quaint confines of St. Johns County.

Garrett was an outsider at the time of his appointment and seemingly was not readily accepted by the clannish community. Thus, it was something of a surprise and upset to many people when Garrett ran for sheriff and was elected in 1972 to remain in office another four years. He won the election although he was not a member of a powerful clique sometimes referred to as "the good ole boys," a group that for years had influenced elections and how things were done in St. Johns County.

During his three years as sheriff, Garrett had been lucky and had run the department without political interference. He had raided the last of the old moonshine stills and put a swift end to cockfighting and other illegal activities that had flourished in the past. He had put Negro deputies in prowl cars for the first time and hired two black detention officers at the St. Johns County Jail, where, before Garrett took over, it was alleged that black prisoners had been mistreated.

At the time of Athalia's murder, some parents in the community were pressuring Garrett to start moving against the drug traffic that had mushroomed while he concentrated on other ills. He had set up a "Turn in Pushers" hot line which already had resulted in a number of arrests. Meantime, he was haunted by a gut feeling that despite his progress in righting some of the wrongs in the county, people still lacked confidence in the ability of local law enforcement agencies to put murderers behind bars.

He made a silent pledge that the Lindsley death would not be added to the list of unsolved murders in his files. He was tired of people mocking the police, alleging, for example, that anyone with $500 could hire a hit man in St. Johns County. He did not believe for a minute that Athalia had been executed by a hired killer.

The afternoon of the day Athalia was killed, Garrett went out of town right after lunch and was still away when Locke McCormick called the police that evening. There were people, including the victim's husband, who were of the opinion that, had Garrett been on hand to respond to Locke's call, the murder scene might have been better secured.

Unfortunately, emergency technicians were first on the scene, and one of them, sickened by the sight of so much blood, had grabbed a garden hose and flooded the porch and steps and walkway, possibly washing away bloody footprints or other evidence that could have helped in identifying the killer. There were other blunders and errors in judgment in that first crucial hour after the murder. Sgt. Francis O'Loughlin and Sgt. Joe Larrow, the first city police officers on the scene, went immediately into the house, hands on their hip pistols, ready to draw in the event the killer was hiding there. Before back up officers arrived, the yard was aswarm with people who seemed to have suddenly dropped out of the sky.

No one had covered Athalia's slashed body or made an effort to block the scene to public access when James Lindsley arrived and, in an indignant outburst, cursed the police for not showing "more respect for the dead." Later, in a conversation with Garrett, he would refer to activity at the scene that evening as "a comedy of errors." "The beast (Athalia's killer) probably got away while the police were tracking blood through the house," he said.

But, as Sgt. O'Loughlin would later testify in court, the officers made the house search before talking to Locke McCormick who could have told them he saw the killer exiting the scene, disappearing around the corner of the house.

Garrett personally saw no humor in the situation when he arrived at eight-thirty, more than two hours after the murder, and people unauthorized to be there were still milling around in the yard. The sheriff chomped moodily on an unlit cigar as O'Loughlin and other officers briefed him on what had transpired. Every available officer in the police department had been called to comb the neighborhood in an intense effort to find the killer and the murder weapon. Police had rifled through every garbage can and every shrub for two solid blocks north and south of the house. The victim's husband had helped establish that nothing of value was missing from the house, ruling out robbery as a motive. Officers had talked to many of the neighbors in addition to the McCormicks and Lucille Smith, hoping to find an eyewitness to the murder. If anyone had witnessed the slaying, Locke was the only one admitting it. He had provided investigators' with their only description of the killer.

The McCormick family was extremely shaken and both Rosemary and her mother, Mrs. Smith, expressed fear for Locke's life, pleading with investigators to withhold his name when they were questioned by the news media.

After talking with the McCormicks, Police Officers O'Loughlin and Larrow had gone immediately to the Stanford home. They were questioning Mrs. Stanford and her teen-age daughter, Patricia, when Alan Stanford drove into the parking area at the rear of the house.

Although Patti and Patricia would not admit it, O'Loughlin believed both had witnessed the murder. He said they had looked at Alan with questioning eyes, big as saucers, when he stepped out of the car.

O'Loughlin also believed Stanford already knew what had happened before he was told his neighbor had been murdered.

The officers had confronted Stanford with the information that a trail of blood droplets, leading from the dead woman's body, appeared to have come to a dead end on his property, and demanded an account of his where-abouts that evening.

At one point during the interrogation, O'Loughlin said he believed Stanford was about to admit to knowing something about the murder when a police department superior interrupted and ordered O'Loughlin and Larrow back to the scene of the crime. O'Loughlin said Stanford was more composed when he questioned him much later in the evening. O'Loughlin had advised him he had the right to remain silent and consult an attorney and he appeared to have done so.

O'Loughlin told Garrett he believed the interrup-tion had prevented the officers' getting a confession from Stanford.

Garrett listened intently and refrained from commenting on procedures that were followed. Later on, he took a flashlight from his car and walked around the yard, shining the beam in all directions, looking for anything the police might have missed. He retraced the trail of blood droplets discovered earlier, trying to determine exactly where the trail stopped. He found what appeared to be the last spot of blood outside the garage of the Stanford home. Initial police reports released to the news media, said the blood stopped at shrubs that were growing over a three-foot concrete wall that separated the Lindsley and Stanford property.

After the last of the city police crew had departed, Garrett stood alone in the shadows of budding azaleas that landscaped the front of Athalia's house, trying to piece together all that had happened that evening. Standing there, he heard a door slam and observed the figure of a man who walked across the front porch of the Stanford home and out into the yard toward the concrete wall. The glow from a street light enabled Garrett to recognize the angular facial features of Alan Stanford as he walked the depth of the yard from front to back several times. Stanford walked slowly, his head bent as though looking for something on the ground.

It had been a stressful afternoon and evening for the county manager. Everything possible had gone wrong. He had told the police he had come home about 5:15 that afternoon and changed into old clothes to do some work on the house--it was old and always in need of repairs--when it dawned on him he had forgotten to sign some important papers his secretary had put on his desk to be mailed. So, he decided to return to the office to get them ready for mailing. Stanford said he left without supper about 5:45. He hadn't checked his watch but he estimated that he got to the office a few minutes before six and stayed about forty minutes.

Stanford said he had forgotten about the letters mainly because of unexpected visitors who had come to his office around four-thirty that afternoon. Two investigators from the Florida Board of Professional Engineers and Land Surveyors had come to advise the county manager of a complaint they'd received that he was misrepresenting himself as a licensed engineer by affixing the title "county engineer" under his signature on important county documents. The investigators had warned him he must cease the practice or he could be in serious trouble with the state. Stanford said the men didn't tell him who had signed the complaint.

Watching Stanford as he paced back and forth in the yard, Garrett, resisted an impulse to subject him to another round of questioning that evening. Instead, he went to a phone and called Shannon Smith.

Garrett said he had seen Shannon getting into the car with Athalia at noon. "I wondered if she was worried or upset about anything? Did she mention being threatened by anyone?"

"No, she didn't mention being afraid of anyone but she made quite an issue at lunch about not using knives today. She said it was bad luck to use knives of any kind on the Chinese New Year," Shannon said.

"How very odd," Garrett said finally after a thoughtful silence.

Chapter 6

The Last Hell Raising

On Tuesday, January 22, the day before she was murdered, Athalia Ponsell Lindsley bristled into an afternoon session of the St. Johns County Commission to raise more hell about County Manager Alan Stanford.

Athalia's eyes swept the room like a broom, checking for familiar faces, reporters like Shannon Smith in particular, before focusing an icy stare on County Manager Stanford, who sat alone at a table near the commissioners' elevated seats, smoking a cigarette and shuffling through a stack of papers. Stanford glared back at Athalia through a haze of smoke, his jaw bone twitching.

The four commissioners present squirmed uneasily in their swivel chairs as Athalia took a seat near the front of the commission chambers amid about a dozen people who had come to complain about an experimental road paving project. As Athalia found a seat among the gathering, the ice in her green eyes melted. She smiled and nodded approvingly at the folks around her. In her travels around the county, she had spotted the cracked paving on their road and had spent a full day discussing their problems with them. Some of the residents already had been contemplating asking county commissioners for help before she helped convince them they should make a formal complaint. She couldn't take all of the credit for their being there, but she was none the less encouraged by the turnout. The size was even better than she had been led to expect.

Commissioners observed her expressions like mice watching a cat, silently wishing they were in Mexico with their absent fellow board member, County Commission Chairman, Fred Green.

It was Athalia's fifth trip before the board since Stanford had failed to pass a state examination that would have licensed him as a civil engineer in Florida. Passing the exam was a condition for his permanent employment commissioners had stipulated when they hired him in 1972 to replace a highly qualified civil engineer who had resigned to take a more lucrative job. The majority of board members wanted someone with qualifications as good if not better than those of the man they had lost. But, Stanford managed to convince three of the five commissioners that his degree in marine engineering would provide him with sufficient background to make it possible for him to pass the state examination required for certification as a civil engineer. He had said he was willing to take night courses, if necessary, to prepare for the exam. Though he would have preferred that the vote to hire him be unanimous, three votes were all he needed to get the job.

He had agreed to accept a $17,500 a year salary, slightly less than the going rate for civil engineers, and to the board's stipulation that he would not receive a raise until he became certified by the Florida Engineering Board. Until he was certified, he had agreed to use the title of county manager. Athalia was aware of the conditions of his employment, and she was furious because the previous October commissioners had increased Stanford's salary to $20,000 despite his failing the state exam. She had secretly gloated when he failed the test because to her, at least, it was an indication that he was incompetent and had no business supervising county road work.

In previous captious attacks on the balding, grey-haired 49-year-old executive, Athalia had accused him of a little of everything from stealing building supplies from the county road department to falsely signing "county engineer" after his name on important county documents.

Her accusations about the taking of pipe and other county materials had prompted Commissioner Green to ask for an investigation of the matter by the state attorney's office, but nothing came of it. Investigators reported that Stanford had taken pipe for personal use because he was under the impression that it was included in a list of materials the commissioners had declared surplus. Though Stanford had been mistaken, the report cleared him of any intent to steal from the county. Although it was true he had been affixing the title of engineer after his signature on documents, commissioners weren't terribly concerned.

Mostly to appease Athalia, the board had asked him to cease the practice, but he had ignored the commissioners and continued misrepresenting his title on county documents.

In one of her most vicious attacks on Stanford, Athalia had stood up at a meeting, pointed a finger at the county manager and said: "that man threatened to kill me." She also accused him of putting sugar in the gas tank of her old Cadillac, causing a rather large repair bill.

"Sugar?" Stanford had said in a puzzled voice. "What would that do?" The reply had rankled Athalia, but Herbie Wiles, the acting chairman of the commission, stopped her before she could comment on Stanford's ignorance.

,Commissioners refused to discuss the accusations. And, the chairman quickly ruled Athalia out of order, insisting that she sit quietly or leave the meeting. Legitimate complaints were one thing. Character assaults and histrionic outbursts were another. The chairman was aware of the neighborhood spats between Athalia and Stanford and he was determined that county commission chambers would not be turned into a battlefield for settling personal disputes.

In previous appearances before the board, Athalia had spoken without support from other spectators. But, on that day before her death, things were different. The dozen or so residents of Joe Ashton Road, sitting around her, shared her disenchantment with Stanford and county road work. Members of the delegation were prepared to say so as the hearing, scheduled first on the agenda, began.

The Joe Ashton road delegation had two specific complaints. The first had to do with an unsuccessful experimental paving project Stanford had undertaken along the rural road. If it had been successful, he planned to use the same type of paving in other areas. But, after two months, the surface had begun to crack like an egg and some of the cracks were deepening into ruts.

Residents who spoke that afternoon told commissioners that Stanford had admitted "he goofed" but was doing nothing to correct the problem. Instead, he had launched another experimental project on 50 acres of privately owned land at the dead end of Joe Ashton Road. The new project involved the dumping and composting of tons and tons of smelly garbage at the site. The theory behind the project was that the waste would act as fertilizer for pine seedlings that would eventually be planted by the paper manufacturing company that owned the acreage. Composting the garbage also would eliminate the need for the county to open a new landfill.

Residents complained that the use of heavy trucks to haul garbage to the site twice daily was worsening the condition of the road and that the stench from the rotting garbage was so nauseating and the garbage was attracting so many flies, they could no longer sit on their porches. The residents said they had spoken to Stanford about the problem on a number of occasions and they were fed up with being ignored, which was why they were appealing to the commission.

Chief spokesperson for the Joe Ashton delegation was Clyde Woolover, a sawed-off little man with a leathery, wind-burned face. Woolover had taken time off from his job of running a road grader for St. Johns County to advise the commissioners that their manager, and his boss, Alan Stanford, was not knowledgeable about road building. He said Stanford was not qualified for his job and that the county was suffering, Woolover told the commission. "The condition of Joe Ashton and other roads in the county is deplorable," he said.

"What background do you have that qualifies you to judge Mr. Stanford's qualifications?" The question was posed by Commissioner Richard Parks, who held a degree in civil engineering from Georgia Tech.

Woolover said he had worked for a number of years building roads for the National Park Service. "The federal government would never permit the kind of shoddy work that's going on in this county," he added.

When Woolover sat down, Athalia Lindsley bolted up to the speakers' podium with an "I told you so" look on her face. Her hands danced with excitement and she glared at Stanford as she began speaking.

"I am a citizen and a taxpayer of St. Johns County and I demand once and for all to know what experience the county manager has had that would qualify him for the work he is doing."

Stanford flushed a deep purple and sprang to his feet to begin listing his degrees in marine engineering and business administration. In addition, he said he had worked nearly a decade for an aircraft manufacturing plant in Baltimore, Maryland and later for the same industry in St. Augustine.

"You haven't answered the question," Athalia shot back. "What does a marine engineer know about building roads? He's putting taxpayers' money down a rat hole," she shouted over the bang of the chairman's gavel.

The Joe Ashton Road residents applauded loudly. Ignoring the gavel, Athalia continued, looking directly at the four members of the county board. "It's high time you gentleman replaced Mr. Stanford with a civil engineer. Give this county what it deserves."

Three of the commissioners looked uneasy but Acting Chairman Herbie Wiles sidestepped the issue, passing off Mrs. Lindsley's comments as an attempt "to settle a personal vendetta."

Woolover and other members of the Joe Ashton delegation had provided ammunition for Athalia's campaign to get Stanford fired and apparently had jarred the county manager's usual composure. Leaping to his feet, he asked the chairman's permission "to ask her a question."

But, Wiles was determined to end the diatribe. "I can't permit a personality conflict to be aired in these chambers," he ruled. "If you have anything else to discuss, I suggest you and Mrs. Lindsley step outside."

Stanford uttered a muted sigh, said, "I pass," and sat down. But he was visibly annoyed.

Athalia had then trotted out of the room in a huff but commissioners knew better than to hope they had heard the last of her.

Stanford sat smouldering, watching Athalia's exit, too angry to feel relief and then turned glassy eyes on Woolover. The next day Woolover's foreman fired him for absences from his job, but Athalia Lindsley would not live long enough to hear about it.

Chapter 7

The Bluejay Did It

For nearly a week after the murder, curiosity over what direction the investigation was taking was fed mostly by rumors that flew like kites on a windy day.

Except for releasing the results of the autopsy performed on Athalia's body, Garrett had put members of the news media on hold. There was nothing unexpected in the medical examiner's report, confirming that Athalia had been literally hacked to death and nearly decapitated. The doctor had found cut marks and slashes all over the dead woman's body and was of the opinion that the knife used by the killer was a machete.

The murder weapon was the subject of the first street corner and barber shop gossip circulated the morning after the murder. An employee at the road and bridge department leaked the story that a machete Alan Stanford had checked out in December was missing and that Garrett had called Stanford to his office for questioning. Road department employees also leaked information that Garrett had found blood stains on the front seat of the county-owned Chevrolet Impala Stanford had been driving the previous evening and had impounded the vehicle.

A story spread quickly that after meeting with Garrett, Stanford had not returned to the office because County Commissioners had violated the Florida Sunshine Law, met in secret, and suspended the county manager pending the results of the murder investigation.

Garrett refused to comment to reporters on any of the rumors but when Shannon Smith called County Commission Chairman Herbie Wiles, he squashed the story that the board had suspended Stanford. There had been no meeting, secret or otherwise, he said. Garrett questioned Alan as a matter of routine. "Poor guy was naturally a little shaken up so I gave him the day off," Wiles said.

Wiles also said any one of the five county commissioners, who were Stanford's employers, could have excused him from work without calling a meeting and that he was personally convinced that "poor Alan had nothing whatsoever to do with the terrible death of Mrs. Lindsley. It is terrible to be innocent and not know how to defend yourself. I personally think the sheriff should be looking in other directions."

There were others of that same opinion.

Some people who lived in or near the Marine Street neighborhood were upset because sheriff's deputies were going door to door, displaying a black and white photograph of the Chevrolet Impala Stanford drove on the night of the murder. Specifically, the deputies wanted to know if anyone had seen the car in the neighborhood around the time Athalia was murdered. Virginia King, a resident of Charlotte Street, was positively indignant because deputies were not showing pictures of any other cars. "It's obvious that Sheriff Garrett is trying to pin this murder on poor Alan. Otherwise, why isn't Dudley showing us pictures of Jim Lindsley's car? Jinx is no angel. Everyone knows how badly he treated his first wife," Virginia complained to one of the reporters who canvassed Athalia's neighbors for information the day after the murder.

Friday morning, January 25, Alan Stanford returned to his office. His wife, driving the family car, dropped him off. Stanford walked by a group of road department mechanics without speaking. Later that day, his secretary, Hazel McCallum confided to Garrett that Stanford had come to work in a "black mood," and had found fault with almost everything she did. The cup of freshly brewed coffee she handed him was too strong. He had insisted that she perk another pot and retype two letters. Several phone calls that came in from reporters had not improved his mood. He had refused to answer any of their questions. "Something about that man terrifies me," Hazel told Garrett.

Chief Virgil Stuart was the only official giving information to reporters that day. The main word from Stuart, or "the biggie" as the press sarcastically put it, was that Stuart was turning over the city's part in the investigation to Police Sgt. Dominic Nicklo who would work as a two-man team with Sheriff Garrett. But, on the heels of that announcement, the chief told Ivan Perry, a reporter representing a radio station, that "the trail is cold."

Later that day, Chief Stuart, for some unexplainable reason, threw out a final crumb to Shannon Smith, which she used to write a human interest-type story for the *Florida Times-Union*. She said later that her editor's only reason for running the silly story was to keep the murder in the news while the sheriff was keeping a tight lid on hard facts related to the investigation. Her story quoted Stuart as saying, Athalia's bluejay, Clementine, may have been the only eyewitness to its mistress' brutal death.

Stuart made the statement after telling the reporter that the police had found bird feathers, resembling those of a bluejay, in Athalia's yard near the beginning of the trail of blood left by the killer.

A few days after the inane story appeared, Shannon received in the mail a picture of a bluejay with a hand-printed message: "Tell Dudley the bluejay did it."

About that same time, a volunteer at the St. Augustine Humane Society confided to Shannon, "off the record," that Garrett had impounded Stanford's pet cat at the shelter. She said the sheriff had taken samples of the cat's hair and sent them to the crime lab in Tallahassee in an effort to determine if the fur from the Stanford's cat matched hair found on Athalia's blood stained clothes and other animal hair found in the vehicle Stanford was driving the night of the murder. Garrett would never confirm or deny the cat story nor say what the comparison of the hair might prove. But, the story is significant only in that it is typical of some of the puzzling information that was passed in the aftermath of the murder.

On Saturday following the murder, the fickle grapevine shifted its focus on possible suspects from Alan Stanford to James Lindsley. Someone had observed men digging in Lindsley's yard on Lew Boulevard and immediately jumped to the conclusion the men were investigators, looking for Jim's machete. Actually the men were Sears employees, digging post holes to install a fence around the Lindsley property.

The conclusion that Jim had buried a machete in his yard was wrong but it was true that Jim Lindsley was no longer carrying around a machete in the back of his station wagon. The fact was that Garrett had confiscated the machete but in responding to reporters' questions about that rumor, Garrett said only that a number of machetes and other types of knives had been turned in or handed over to investigators. He declined to say how or from whom the weapons were acquired. Then, on Monday after the murder, it became apparent that the search for the knife used on Athalia had not ended.

Early in the day sheriff's deputies began standing vigil along the banks of Maria Sanchez Lake to watch a city work crew begin pumping water from the lake and draining it into a nearby swamp. The lake is located about a block south of Athalia's home and Garrett ordered it drained on a hunch that Athalia's killer might have tossed in the weapon as he fled from the murder scene. The lake flows southward between Cordova Street and South Street. It was no secret that South Street was on the route Stanford normally took when he drove to and from his Marine Street home and his office. Although officials told the press the lake draining was just routine maintenance, and unrelated to the murder, no one was fooled by that story.

The hum of the pumps continued all of Monday and Monday night. It was late Tuesday afternoon before the lake's sandy bottom was completely exposed and a parade-sized crowd stood watching as deputies began to scavenge through the assortment of litter collected in the 10 or more years since the lake had undergone cleaning. There was no mistaking the disappointment on officers' faces as they plowed through a graveyard of rusty cans, bottles, soggy candy wrappers, popsicle sticks, sunken toys, much the same variety of debris one finds in drainage ditches and wooded areas.

Though Garrett pegged the lake draining as an "exercise in futility," he already was devising another plan to find the weapon. One that would prove more productive.

Chapter 8

The Silence of Fear

Sheriff Garrett would have bet his badge that someone other than Locke McCormick had seen Athalia Lindsley's killer. Yet, there almost seemed to be a conspiracy of silence in the Marine Street neighborhood as Garrett and a team of investigators went door to door asking questions after the murder.

Garrett said later that he strongly suspected fear played a part in the silence. Everyone on the street knew Rosemary McCormick was terrified that her son's life was in danger because of all the publicity naming him as "the only eyewitness." Some of Rosemary's friends shared her irritation with the police for releasing Locke's name to reporters.

Because of the unusual brutality of the crime, supposition that a maniac might be loose on the town was understandable. Patti Stanford specifically expressed that fear to police the night of the murder. But, it puzzled Garrett, that despite what she had said, Mrs. Stanford had made no effort to stop her teen-age daughter, Patricia, from driving off alone in the family's Lincoln Continental about an hour after the murder, through the shadowy, dimly lit streets, to a teen-age meeting.

Fear was not the only snag to the investigation. More than once in his conversations with Athalia's neighbors, Garrett was nagged by the feeling that they didn't much care whether or not Athalia's killer was caught because Athalia had been such a disruptive force in the neighborhood. Garrett was a veteran lawman and a realist. The killer had silenced a neighborhood menace forever. Ironically, Athalia's death had created another kind of disruption. Garrett sensed that some of the neighbors, including the McCormicks, resented the sudden intrusion of police, reporters and an unprecedented number of "sightseers" almost as much as they had resented Athalia. Indirectly, that too, was her fault. Marine Street was not a part of the approved route for trailer-trains and horse-drawn sightseeing carriages but that had not stopped tourists who read about the murder from finding the street on their own and walking or driving by the house.

For a solid week the neighborhood was stripped of any degree of privacy by strangers asking questions, taking pictures, or just standing around whispering and pointing.

Oddly, Patti Stanford and her family appeared to be the least affected by the intrusions. The day after the murder, when police began the questioning of neighbors, they found Mrs. Stanford entertaining her bridge club.

They also found the Rev. Michael Boss, the rector of Trinity Episcopal Parish where the Stanford and the McCormick families attended, leaving the Stanford home. Outside, Shannon Smith asked Boss what he was doing there and also how Mrs. Stanford was doing.

The minister replied, "She's okay. I just thought I would drop in because they are members of our church."

"Do you know anything you are not telling me?" Shannon asked.

Boss's answer was a shrug which led Shannon to believe he probably did. Of course, later on, rumors began circulating that Stanford had given a full confession to the Rev. Boss because he knew Boss never would be required to testify to anything told him in the confessional.

Frances Bemis, a 70-year-old woman who lived four doors down the street from Athalia's house, was perhaps the only neighbor who didn't seem to resent any of the disruptions. She talked freely to anyone who came by. When Sheriff's Capt. R.M. "Red" Williams rang her bell, she opened the door and immediately invited him inside, literally beaming. Anyone sent from Garrett was welcome, she said. As a sheriff, Garrett was tops in her book.

Other people on Marine Street had voted for Garrett but other than that, Marine Street residents had little else in common with Mrs. Bemis. It did not especially bother Frances that the Maria Sanchez Apartment House she ran to supplement her retirement income was not as luxurious as some of the other homes on the street. Because her house was at the south end of the street, far enough away from the fancier structures with their sculptured hedges and manicured lawns, residents over-looked the lack of pride she took in her yard.

She had turned the two story house into apart-ments and half of the front yard served as an unpaved parking area for her tenants' automobiles. Grass grew in shaggy patches on the other half. Leggy-looking gerani-ums with yellowing leaves, sprouting from urns flanking her front entrance were the only sign of flowers in the yard. Frances made no apologies, except to say she had "a black thumb." But, in an impulsive attempt to brighten the drab facade, she had recently painted her front door lavender.

Frances had different values than most of her neighbors. She was more impressed with the talents and the philosophies of people she met than by their social status. She was intrigued by people like Athalia Ponsell Lindsley.

"Do come in," she said, ushering Williams through a drab hallway and into the more attractive living room of her downstairs apartment. She offered him a seat on the chintz sofa and noticing the cigars in the breast pocket of his sports coat, she pointed to a king-sized ash tray on the marble-topped coffee table, inviting him to smoke.

Williams looked grateful. The majority of folks he talked to--women especially--hated the smell of cigars, much more so than smoke from cigarettes.

Right away Frances told him how much she had liked Athalia and how pleased she was that the police and the newspapers were giving her murder so much attention. She thought she might be the only neighbor who had really liked the dead woman except for Jean Troemel, Jim Lindsley's artist friend, who lived around the corner on

South Street. Frances said she had rather approved of Athalia's "meddling" in county politics.

"Athalia was the Ralph Nader of St. Augustine," Frances told Williams.

The officer could hardly believe his ears. The odd-looking little woman with henna colored hair and slanted Oriental eyes was full of surprises.

Williams listened attentively as Frances explained that her friendship with Athalia had developed suddenly, just a week prior to the murder. She said Jean Troemel had invited Frances and Athalia to a luncheon. The two women had quickly discovered they had much in common; many parallels in their lives. Both women had enjoyed successful careers in New York City. Frances had worked as a fashion coordinator for Abraham Strauss during a portion of the same period that Athalia had been a Powers model. Both Frances and Athalia had weathered three unsuccessful, childless marriages. They had shared a voracious interest in fashion, art, music, and the theater. Both women had nursed their mothers through terminal illnesses and both were animal lovers and champions of causes.

Frances had demonstrated for civil right, marching with the blacks when Martin Luther King had come to St. Augustine in the early 60's. She had demonstrated an ongoing concern over the treatment of the horses that marched along St. Augustine streets, pulling sightseeing carriages. She was convinced that the horses were over-worked and underfed and that some of them needed medical attention.

She was one of the first of a number of people to complain to the Humane Society when one of the horses collapsed from a heat stroke while touring along Avenida Menendez in the summer of 1973. Though she had raised her share of eyebrows, Frances was a little better liked in St. Augustine than Athalia.

However, Frances told Williams that she also had been involved in a dispute with Alan Stanford, but the dispute was unrelated to the problems between Athalia and the county manager. Frances' confrontation with Stanford occurred before she had met Athalia and sprang from her disapproval of the way Stanford was treating his pet Labrador.

It was her opinion that the dogs were neglected. More than once, Frances had observed one of the animals barely escape being struck by a car. When it rained, the dogs often took shelter on Frances' front porch. Usually, she toweled the dogs dry and gave them something to eat. Although she had no pets of her own, Frances always kept a supply of cat and dog food to feed strays. She also bought pet food to donate to the Humane Society.

One rainy afternoon she decided to confront Stanford about why he did not provide better shelter for his animals. Frances said her advice was not well received and the conversation had ended with Stanford telling her the welfare of his dogs was none of her business.

Williams listened patiently to Frances' ramblings before finally getting around to the purpose of his visit and asking what she had seen or heard on the night Athalia was killed.

"I understand you take a walk every evening about six," he prompted.

Frances nodded, relating that she had left for her walk a little later than usual the night of the murder. A phone call had delayed her. She had just locked the front door and started out when an ambulance came streaking up the street.

She said she watched to see where the ambulance was going and then walked up the street, wondering if Athalia was ill.

"It crossed my mind she might have had a stroke--like her mother. I intended to find out what was wrong."

As a result, Frances said she was one of the first people on the street to see Athalia lying there on the walk in a river of blood.

"It was horrible beyond belief," she said.

"You didn't happen to get a glimpse of the man who did it?" Williams asked.

"Nooo . . . there was no one in the yard but the ambulance boys," Frances said.

"Have you any idea who might have done it?"

Frances was suddenly silent. She thought for a moment before answering.

"I would not want to finger anyone but everyone knows Athalia had made some enemies."

Williams squinted at Frances through a cloud of cigar smoke, not pressing for a name. Then, he held up the picture of Stanford's Chevrolet Impala.

"Did you see this car anywhere the night Mrs. Lindsley was killed?"

"No, but I have seen it in the neighborhood many times," she replied.

Williams sighed. "I guess you know if you had started walking a little earlier, you probably would have witnessed the murder."

"Yes," she replied with a shudder. "I've thought a lot about that."

Minutes after Williams left, Phil Green, a reporter from Miami, rang Frances Bemis' doorbell. Again she described her walk up Marine Street on the night of the murder and the horror of seeing her neighbor's body, butchered like an animal.

Mostly, the reporter wanted to know if she feared for her own life. A Jacksonville newspaper had reported that the entire neighborhood was terrified. Did she think a maniac was on the loose?

Frances said she was not the least bit afraid and had taken her usual evening walk the night of the murder. That was not exactly true. Actually, Frances had started on her walk, gone as far as Athalia's and returned home where she called two friends in Flagler County, begging them to come and spend the night at her house because she was so frightened.

At one point during the discussion about fear, Frances had laughed, recalling that she had walked alone in the evening for many years, even when she lived in New York City.

"I've never been afraid and certainly not in St. Augustine. It is one of the safest places I've ever lived. Besides, who would bother an old woman like me?"

Most certainly, Frances said, she did not suspect a maniac was on the loose.

"The killer was only after Athalia. He was someone who hated her very much."

Chapter 9

Murder Suspects Confirmed

About a week after Athalia Lindsley's murder, Garrett lost his battle to keep a lid on the direction the investigation was taking when a Jacksonville television station issued a report, naming both former Mayor James Lindsley and County Manager Alan Stanford as suspects in her death.

Anchormen reported that the homes of both men had been searched, a machete owned by Lindsley had been confiscated, and the county car Stanford was driving on the evening of the murder had been impounded. The car was sent to Tallahassee, along with one of the victim's fingers, dismembered during the attack, for the purpose of determining if blood that left stains on the front seat of Stanford's car was the same as that of the victim.

At first, Garrett was angry. Technically the report clearly violated the civil rights of both Stanford and Lindsley. Neither had been legally accused nor charged in the murder. At the onset of the investigation, Garrett had issued an order that no one in the sheriff's department was to answer any reporter's questions concerning suspects or other aspects of the investigation. There were to be no exceptions including his own son-in-law, Ron Sachs, a reporter the *Miami Herald* had sent to St. Augustine.

Garrett suspected that someone in his department had violated his order. But, he knew, as did Lindsley and Stanford, that the distasteful television report was really nothing more than an echo of information, already wide-spread by the town wags.

The invasion of privacy was one of the penalties of living in a small, fish-bowl type community like St. Augustine, which at that time, had less than 14,000 residents, many of whom were related by birth or mar-riage. The legally mandated veil of secrecy intended to protect suspects in an investigation was something of a joke. Privacy was not a commodity in the oldest city in the United States. Gossiping was the favorite indoor sport and Athalia's body was scarcely cold before the town became polluted with rumors and speculation.

With an ear at every keyhole, by the time the television report was aired, most people not only already knew Lindsley and Stanford were being investigated and, fair or not, many residents had pretty much decided which one was guilty--or to be more accurate--which man they wanted to be guilty.

The murder had caused the town to split like an over ripe watermelon. Half of the people involved in the fracture were saying Lindsley had killed his wife--probably in a drunken, senseless rage; the other half believed that Stanford had hacked his neighbor to death in a fit of revenge for the problems she was causing him.

Those people who fingered Lindsley as the killer based their suspicions mostly on stories that indicated, in their minds at least, that he was a violent man, who drank hard liquor and lots of it and had frequently physically abused his first wife, Lillian. One juicy rumor was that on at least one occasion he had punched his new wife, Athalia, in the eye. Supposedly, Jim had given Athalia a black eye during an argument over a contribution she had intended to mail to a television evangelist. According to the story, Athalia had discovered that Jim intercepted the letter with the contribution and had destroyed the contribution check. It was true that Athalia had eaten lunch at Seafair, wearing dark glasses, everyday for nearly a week the month before the murder.

Despite his faults, Jim had managed to attract and marry two beautiful women--near look alikes--both slender, long-stemmed blondes with exceptionally handsome bone structure and both had been professionally trained dancers. For years, Lillian had been the owner of a dance studio where she also taught ballet and tap dancing. Lillian was far better liked than Athalia. Even people who disliked Lindsley were fond of Lillian who was every inch a lady, gentle and sensitive to other people's feelings and needs; never critical or judgmental. She wasn't one to whine or complain about her marriage but more than one of her dance students had carried home stories that Mrs. Lindsley had come to class with bruises showing on her face and arms and legs.

No one was surprised when after the older of Jim and Lillian's two sons was killed in a motorcycle accident and his younger brother had gone away to college, Lillian finally asked Jim for a divorce and he agreed.

However, the couple remarried two years later.

Many of Lillian's friends still blamed Lindsley for the traffic accident in which Lillian suffered a broken neck and was killed. They called the police report that absolved Jim from blame a "St. Augustine white wash." They said "politics" had saved him and that it wasn't the first time law enforcement had covered for a city official.

Some City Hall wags gave voice to some outrageous stories of how Lindsley made it a common practice to take advantage of his office. They said, for example, that during the time he served on the city commission, he was never billed for water. And, when a big issue was at stake, he was not above selling his vote to the highest bidder.

It was rather amazing that in view of the slanderous things people were saying about Lindsley and the willingness to hang Athalia's death on him that he ever had garnered the votes to be elected to four three-year terms on the city commission and that he was twice chosen to serve as mayor.

Some of the stories circulating about Lindsley were more humorous than vicious. Like the one involving a time, when as mayor, he was asked to cut the ribbon at the opening of Jax Liquor Store on King Street in St. Augustine. When he didn't show up at the opening ceremony, a store executive called to ask if he had forgotten his promise. Jim said he had not forgotten but he had no intention of cutting the ribbon until Jax sent out the complimentary case of Scotch the store owner had promised. As the story went, he did not show up for the ribbon cutting until after the case of Scotch was sent by taxi to his home.

Not all of the people who disliked Lindsley were part of the segment that believed he had killed Athalia. It was not that they believed him incapable of murder. They said hacking someone to death was not his style. Lindsley had a history of fighting with his fists. One rumor was that he had nearly beaten a man to death at one time. But, never, ever had anyone ever known him to go after Lillian or anyone else with a knife.

There also were strong feelings even among people who disapproved of Lindsley that Alan Stanford had a far stronger reason than the former mayor to want Athalia dead.

As far as anyone knew, Athalia had posed no threat to Lindsley. But, she was a decided threat to Stanford's professional integrity. She was making his life miserable both at home and at work. She had said abusive things to his face and to his back. She had frequently used the Southern expression "poor white trash" in referring to Stanford and his family. In a public meeting, she had called him a liar, and accused him of threatening to kill her. She had left no doubt in anyone's mind that she would leave no stone unturned in her crusade to get him fired from his job.

Stanford had turned 49 a few days after Athalia's murder. At his age, there was no guarantee he could find another position that would allow him to continue the Cadillac lifestyle that he and his social minded wife so much enjoyed.

James Lindsley was a native son, born in the three-story coquina house on St. George Street where his father, Dr. Horace Lindsley, a respected physician, had practiced medicine when Jim was growing up. But Stanford, like Athalia, was a newcomer. He had lived in St. Augustine less than five years. But unlike Athalia, he had scored socially. He was a member of the elite Rod and Gun Club and he was invited to all of the important city and county functions. His wife played bridge with members of some of the oldest, most important families. His daughters played tennis with their kids.

Stanford was something of a split personality if you compared his popularity in social circles with his unpopular status at work. If the rumblings were true, the majority of his employees either feared or resented him.

The minutes of one county commission meeting reflected that county commissioners had devoted the entire session to hearing the complaints about Stanford presented by a longtime employee and road department supervisor, Pete Hardeman, who attested, as had Athalia, that Stanford was not suited for his job as county manager and was creating a morale problem among employees of the road and bridge department. That meeting came about as a result of Stanford's trying to fire Hardeman and was held a year before Athalia had entered the picture. Nothing much had come of it except some newspaper publicity about the internal squabbling in the county road department. Commissioners urged Stanford to make more of an effort to get along with the older employees and then promptly let the matter drop. The bottom line was most of the commissioners really liked Alan Stanford.

As for credibility in the Christian community, Stanford had one big advantage over Lindsley. He went to church regularly. He knelt for morning prayer in one of the front pews at Trinity Parish and took communion at the altar rail almost every Sunday. Lindsley usually went hunting on Sunday morning. He supposedly was a Presbyterian but he didn't often go to church.

At the time of Athalia's murder, Stanford was serving as a member of the vestry at Trinity Episcopal Parish, the oldest non-Roman church in Florida, and one of the most majestic churches in the city.

The election of a newcomer to the Trinity Parish vestry was practically unheard of at that time. People from very old and very well-heeled families ran the church like a country club. Many visitors were snubbed right out the front door. Episcopalians who wanted to transfer from other parishes really needed an invitation and an introduction from an established member to feel comfortable attending services.

The country club atmosphere prevailed at church suppers and other events which often were preceded by tailgate cocktail parties in the church parking lot.

During the three or so years the Rev. Michael Boss had been rector, he had made every effort to change attitudes, and stressed the need to communicants how important it was to make newcomers feel welcome, but, the icy atmosphere continued.

Stanford and his family had been properly introduced by several longtime communicants. With minimal efforts, Stanford had inched his way into the inner sanctum of the rigid power structure of the city and the old church.

Even before Stanford became a murder suspect, the Rev. Boss had experienced private moments of regret that Stanford was part of the vestry. He was not as easy going and cooperative as Boss had expected. He tended to be argumentive and nit-picking at meetings. Boss was beginning to wonder if the Southern gentlemanly type of charm Stanford had previously exhibited was just a veneer.

Once Stanford became a suspect, Boss dispensed with his personal feelings and extended a full measure of spiritual support to Stanford and his family.

As for the communicants, many were outraged that Garrett would dare to treat someone from their elite fold as a murder suspect. Others were much more concerned that a man they had entrusted to represent them on the vestry, the body that made important decisions in the life of the historical church, might indeed have committed one of the most heinous crimes of the century. Some of them wished Stanford would step down until such time as his name was cleared.

Boss privately agreed it would be the prudent thing for Stanford to do. But, the priest was not about to suggest it. It would imply a lack of faith in Stanford's innocence. So, Stanford stayed after personally assuring his fellow members of the vestry that he was innocent. He said his feud with Mrs. Lindsley had been "blown out of proportion."

He complained to Boss and again to reporters who covered county commission meetings that Garrett didn't appear to be investigating anyone except him. He accused Garrett of only going through the motions of investigating Lindsley.

"It's me . . . and only me . . . that he's after."
Stanford said.

The county manager had wasted no time engaging
Frank Upchurch Jr., a favorite son of a favorite son, as an
attorney. It came as something of a blow to Garrett that
Upchurch would take the case because he also was
Garrett's attorney.

Chapter 10

Jinx Has A Theory

"Hell, yes, I know I'm a suspect," Jim Lindsley growled.

It was 10 days after the murder and he was sitting in an oak rocker on the front porch of the old family home on St. George Street, smoking an unfiltered cigarette while he talked to Shannon Smith and Dick Hagood, another reporter the *Florida Times-Union* had assigned to assist in coverage of the investigation.

The twisted wrapper of an empty cigarette pack topped the heap of butts in the overflowing ash tray on the writing area of a roll-top antique desk within arm's reach of his chair.

Weather permitting, Lindsley always conducted business on the porch. In addition to the oak desk, the porch had a phone, a file cabinet and three pine rockers with woven seats. The interview was Jim's last appointment on his first day back at the St. George Street office since his wife's death. His coloring was as pasty as that of someone recuperating from a long illness.

Earlier that afternoon, Dick and Shannon were to have interviewed Athalia's sister, Geraldine Horton, who had flown from Honolulu for the funeral and was staying at the house on Marine Street. Sheriff Dudley Garrett was standing at the back gate of Athalia's house when Dick and Shannon arrived. Garrett looked nail-biting angry. He said Geraldine had just refused to see him.

"I hope you have better luck," Garrett told Shannon before impulsively surprising the reporters by removing his badge and handing it to Shannon.

"If she lets you in, show her this, she didn't believe I was who I said I was."

When Shannon hesitated to take the badge, Garrett added, "You can bring it by the office later. I trust you."

A young woman, Shannon later learned was Geraldine's daughter, opened the back door a crack in response to the reporters' knocks. She said Geraldine was resting and did not feel like talking to anyone.

Shannon sighed.

"Well, tell her I was a good friend of her sister's. I only want to help."

"And," Shannon added, "Sheriff Garrett wants her to see this badge. Apparently she didn't believe he was the sheriff. Please bring it back. I have to return it."

Reluctantly, the woman took the badge and left the reporters standing on the back porch while she walked to another part of the house to speak with Geraldine.

A few minutes later, the young woman returned, handed Shannon the badge and asked the reporters to "please leave."

Before closing the door, she said Geraldine did not feel well enough to speak to anyone.

"She will call you later," she said to Shannon.

Earlier, Alan Stanford had refused to be interviewed.

"I shouldn't even tell you my middle name," he said before hanging up the phone on Dick Hagood.

Jim, however, responded to Dick and Shannon's questions with surprising candor.

"This town has been hip-deep in rumors ever since the murder with every God damn story you can think of," Lindsley said testily. "Hell yes, I'm under suspicion and I don't know who else hasn't been. None of this is helping my ulcers. I've been eating these like peanuts," he added, reaching in the breast pocket of his lumberjack shirt for a bottle of pills prescribed for his ulcers.

Lindsley glanced at his watch, observing that it was past five. "I wish I could offer you people a drink. But, I don't keep whiskey here anymore. I have Athalia to thank for that. She convinced me it was bad for my ulcers."

"I guess believing that is hard for some folks to swallow. I used to drive with a fifth between my knees," he added, chuckling. "Poor darling. She never could talk me into quitting these."

As he spoke, he held up a pack of cigarettes he had just removed from a carton in a drawer of the old desk.

"Lord knows, she tried. She even called my doctor in Jacksonville a few days before she was killed and begged him to talk to me about my smoking. He said an astrologist Athalia had been consulting had written her from Miami, warning her that something bad was going to happen."

"Athalia jumped to the conclusion I was going to get lung cancer. That's why she called Dick . . . Dr. Thompson."

Dick and Shannon sat quietly, allowing the white-haired Realtor to continue rambling without interruption. Now and then, Hagood scribbled something in his note-book. Lindsley went on to say it was the first day he had come to his office since Athalia was killed.

"I dreaded it. For--it was right over there beyond that wall that I kissed her goodbye for the last time."

He pointed to the eight-foot coquina rock wall that separated his yard from the municipal parking lot where Athalia had left her car when she drove with Lindsley to Jacksonville the afternoon before she was murdered.

Lindsley rambled on about the trip to Jacksonville and the final stop at a Publix supermarket where he helped his wife select fresh vegetables for the Chinese dinner she had "so looked forward to cooking."

"She was a gourmet cook, you know. The Chinese vegetables are still in my refrigerator. I haven't had the heart or the appetite to try and do anything with them," Lindsley added, gazing reflectively at his hunting dog, a liver-colored pointer asleep on the porch near his chair.

"If she hadn't gone home to feed those dogs of hers, she might still be alive."

Lindsley said he had his own theory of what had happened after Athalia left the parking lot the evening she was killed. "Garrett--the sheriff--and I have been over it a dozen times. He's a good man but he's laboring under an error. A neighbor told him she saw Athalia working in the yard at five-thirty. That's impossible. It was almost five-thirty when we got to the post office."

Jim was of the opinion that Athalia had reached home about 5:35 on the day of her death. He said she had to unlock the back gate and the back door before carrying in the groceries the police found on the kitchen floor.

"Then, she must have gone to the bathroom. She had mentioned having to go real bad when we were at the post office. That would explain why she left the back door open and her keys in the lock. She was a fanatic about keeping that back door locked."

"After going to the bathroom, she probably went out front to get the mail--the police found letters under her body that night. Then, it is my guess she went back and got the bird. She might have been grabbed herself when she grabbed the bird."

Lindsley said Athalia had kept the cage just inside the front door and that the cage had a dent in the side he hadn't recalled seeing until after the murder.

He said the sheriff didn't entirely agree with his theory "because a neighbor claims she saw Athalia with the bird in the yard right before six o'clock. Of course Athalia could have been trying to return the bird to its cage when she was attacked."

Lindsley said he and the sheriff did agree that "the killer was never inside the house."

At that point, Hagood interrupted.

"You just said she might have been grabbed when she reached for the bird."

"What I mean is I don't believe the killer was in any other part of the house except the foyer by the front door. If he had been, it seems logical he would have killed her inside . . . not out there in the open where anyone could see him. There was just no sign other than the dent in the cage of anyone being inside that house." Jim explained.

"Tell me, Mr. Lindsley," Hagood asked suddenly, "Have you any idea who might have killed your wife? Did she have any enemies?"

"Only one," Lindsley answered without hesitation. "She had no enemies except one."

When the *Florida Times-Union* hit the streets the next morning the headline across the top of the front page said: "Lindsley: She Had No Enemies--Except One."

Beneath the headline was Hagood's story quoting Sheriff Garrett as saying that both the husband of the slain Athalia Ponsell Lindsley and the county manager remained on his list of suspects.

The story said "the victim's husband left the distinct impression that he wanted to point his finger at whom he considers to be the killer, though he stopped short of naming names" and that County Manager Stanford had refused to be interviewed or make a statement.

Garrett was quoted as saying that the blood stain found in the county car Alan Stanford drove on the night of the murder had nothing to do with the murder of Athalia Lindsley.

The stain was an old one that had been in the car since Stanford had driven a county employee with an injured, bleeding arm to the hospital months before the murder.

Tests run for the Florida Department of Law Enforcement confirmed that the blood that caused the stain did not match Athalia's blood.

Dick and Shannon had spoken briefly with Garrett twice before going to interview Lindsley--once at the back gate of Athalia's house when Garrett gave Shannon his badge and later when she returned it to his office.

Garrett had refused to talk about the machete, supposedly missing from the county road department or to discuss what, if anything, police had confiscated when they searched Lindsley's and Stanford's residences.

On their own, Dick and Shannon had confirmed that County Judge Charles Mathis had issued a warrant to search Stanford's house. Lindsley told them he had permitted investigators to make an informal search of his home the day after the murder.

"Hell no, I didn't make Garrett get a search warrant. I had nothing to hide," Lindsley said.

For some reason, Lindsley had sidetracked the question when Hagood asked if it were true Garrett had taken his machete at the time of the search."Why don't you ask the sheriff? True, I carry a machete in my car. It comes in handy when I'm showing undeveloped property to clients. I've killed many a snake with it. I'll tell you this much and I hope you quote me. If the SOB that killed my wife used a machete . . . I guarantee you it wasn't mine."

Jim said he had heard the rumor that police had found a machete buried in his yard."Someone who saw the crew from Sears digging post holes for a fence started that silly story."

He said Athalia had talked him into ordering the fence after one of his hunting dogs was struck by a car. "You know how she was about dogs. She thought it was criminal to let them run the streets."

Chapter 11

Stanford Has His Say

Newspaper racks in St. Augustine, containing papers that carried Lindsley's acid comments, emptied before eight o'clock the next morning. The same issue of the *Times-Union* that carried Hagood's interview with Jim, also carried a lengthy mood story by Shannon Smith about the town's reaction to the murder.

The afternoon after the interview with Lindsley appeared in the *Times-Union*, the *St. Augustine Record* pushed ahead in the scavenger hunt for murder-related news by front-paging an exclusive interview with Alan Stanford.

Pat Lynn's story galloped the width of the front page. The eight-column banner head said: "The Pressure Has Been Enormous." Lynn painted County Manager Stanford as a quiet, soft-spoken man, beleaguered by enormous pressures since the murder of his next door neighbor; a man subjected not only to a scapegoat investigation, but also to thick and fast rumors and harassing phone calls.

Stanford was quoted as saying he had been "quite aware" he was a suspect since the day after the murder, and that the pressure on him and his family "has been enormous."

"Now I feel it (the investigation) has gone on long enough and it's time for them (the investigators) to concentrate on other possibilities."

Stanford bemoaned the fact that he was under "a cloud of suspicion." "If you could dispel that idea it would be a public service. . . . I have not been accused . . . if I am accused it is only an accusation. It's not fair I should be a suspect of murder indefinitely."

He regrets, Lynn wrote, "that local lawmen have narrowed the focus of their investigation on him."

Lynn hinted that the Jacksonville news media had contributed to Stanford's anguish.

He wrote: "Last week it was widely and erroneously circulated in St. Augustine that a Jacksonville radio station reported his (Stanford's) arrest. Two days ago a Jacksonville television station broadcast his name as one of two suspects in the case and a Jacksonville newspaper made a similar statement this morning."

Then, came more quotes from Stanford. "I think the investigation has been quite shortsighted . . . they've concentrated their investigation on me because I'm convenient. I can understand that because of the attacks she (Mrs. Lindsley) has made on me. But, there must be a myriad of avenues to study."

The story ended with Stanford saying that he and his family had "shut out" all the publicity linking him to the murder. They had stopped reading the newspaper and watching television news. They had friends sticking by them and according to Stanford "there hasn't been a single failure."

The story carried a one-column picture of the county manager. His mouth was spread in a wide grin.

A few days later on February 6, 1974, the city was preparing to celebrate the birthday of Don Pedro Menendez de Aviles, the Spanish admiral who founded St. Augustine in 1565. The founder's day ceremony was an annual event. That year it was scheduled to take place in the picturesque courtyard of the old Alcazar Hotel, a Henry Flagler-built structure, converted in 1972 for use as a new City Hall.

Spanish flags, flying from poles near the statue of Menendez around which the ceremony would be held, flapped in the chilly breeze. The statue was a recent gift from St. Augustine's sister city of Aviles, Spain.

A flag-draped grandstand had been erected for dignitaries attending the event. Other spectators would sit in folding chairs, borrowed from a funeral home.

James Lindsley was among the former city mayors who had been invited to sit in the grandstand. But, for the first time in years, he was going to miss the festive event.

As dignitaries and their wives began arriving by horse-drawn carriages and Florida's Adjutant General, Henry W. McMillan, prepared to make the welcoming address in Spanish, Lindsley was on his way to keep a 2:00 p.m. appointment at the St. Johns County Court-house just across the street.

The St. Augustine High School band was playing as Lindsley walked up the courthouse steps. The strains of "God Bless America" followed him into the marbled lobby where he took an elevator to the third floor on his way to take a polygraph test.

A few days after Athalia's death, Garrett had asked both Lindsley and Stanford if they would be willing to take a state administered lie detector examination. Garrett explained that results of such tests usually are not admissible in court but they are a good indicator of a suspect's guilt or innocence.

Stanford had refused but Lindsley had agreed to take the test after consulting with his attorney, Robbie Andreu.

On the advice of Andreu, Lindsley had brought along pill bottles containing samples of the prescribed medication he had been taking regularly since his surgery for cancer. The pills would be turned over to the examiner.

Andreu had explained that certain drugs could affect his response to questions during the testing.

Lindsley sat in a chair, rigged with belts and wires connected to the lie detector machine for more than two hours while he answered the same set of questions three times and the examiner watched for changes in his blood pressure, pulse rate and breathing. The changes usually occur when a question is answered untruthfully.

Lindsley was not permitted to smoke during the testing and was suffering for a drag long before the session ended. No matter, he would have done almost anything at that point to try and clear himself of suspicion in his wife's murder. He heaved an exhausted sigh of relief when the questions finally ceased.

"That's it," the examiner smiled, as he freed him from the belts. "Now you can smoke."

"When will I know how I did?" he asked.

"You'll be getting a call from the sheriff later this afternoon," the examiner replied.

Lindsley's eyebrows arched in alarm.

"Don't worry about it," the examiner smiled. "It's just a formality. We always give the results to whoever orders the test."

Lindsley stood a moment, enjoying his cigarette. Then he turned to Andreu.

"Let's go wait in the sheriff's office."

That evening Lindsley called Shannon Smith at home.

"I think you should call the sheriff. He has something interesting to tell you. I could tell you myself but I would rather it come from Dudley."

"Can't you just give me a hint of what it's about?" Shannon asked.

"No, just do as I say. Call Garrett."

The sheriff could not be reached that evening and it was not until 9:00 a.m. the next day that he informed the press that James Lindsley had passed a lie detector test, administered by the Florida Department of Law Enforcement.

"He was tested three times and he gave no indication that he has any knowledge concerning the murder of his wife," Garrett said, adding that "the results of the test have removed James Lindsley from under a cloud of suspicion that has been hovering over his head since the murder."

Garrett said Lindsley's whereabouts at the time of the murder had been substantially documented by the investigators before he agreed to be tested.

At noon on the day after Lindsley passed the test, he met Shannon for lunch at Seafair and poured out his feelings.

"I can't tell you how relieved I feel. These past two weeks have been Hell. I've felt like the loneliest man in the world except for a few staunch and loyal friends who have been a great support."

"I gladly volunteered for the polygraph when Robbie told me the test was available if I didn't object to putting myself in possible jeopardy. I had to sign a statement which said that any results from the test could be used against me."

"In other words, if I had not passed it, I might have been arrested."

Lindsley spoke slowly, pausing frequently to give the reporter time to write down everything he was saying and to interject questions.

Later, Shannon handed him a yellow pad and he wrote out the following statement for the newspaper:

"It is a tremendous relief to have this almost tangible mantle of suspicion removed. This suspicion, compounded with the great grief and loss of a dearly loved one has made the past two weeks horrible to endure."

A waitress had brought his lunch order, but Lindsley continued to write, letting the food cool.

"Now that my name is exonerated, I hope they will begin concentrating on other suspects and find the animal that did it."

Some of Lindsley's excitement over passing the test waned later in the afternoon when the *St. Augustine Record* hit the street.

Lindsley was shocked by the red and white banner headline that screamed at him from across the top of the front page, announcing that both Stanford and Lindsley had passed lie detector tests.

The story beneath said Lindsley's test was administered "yesterday in the county courthouse by an agent of the Florida Department of Law Enforcement," and that Stanford's test was administered "last Wednesday" by a private polygraph examiner called in by his attorney, Frank Upchurch, Jr.

Stanford had released the information about his privately administered polygraph exclusively to the *Record's* reporter, Patrick Lynn.

The story quoted Stanford as saying he was "willing to undertake any reasonable examinations that will assist the authorities in finding Mrs. Lindsley's assailant. I am not guilty and played no part in this horrible event. I am confident that I can pass any impartial polygraph examination."

Stanford said that he passed the privately administered examination before Garrett ever approached him about taking a state administered polygraph.

Garrett read the story, and swore under his breath. It was the first he had heard about Stanford taking a polygraph.

Later, Garrett told a group of reporters that the results of a test administered secretly by a private operator "doesn't carry the weight of an examination by state experts even if the results are immediately turned over to the authorities."

Files in the sheriff's office noted that the test requested by Upchurch was administered to Stanford by a polygraph expert employed by Zales Jewelry Chain. Records also noted that when Lt. Eddie Lightsey asked the Zales examiner if Stanford killed Athalia, the examiner replied: "He said he did not."

Garrett's request to review Stanford's polygraph was denied and Stanford continued to refuse to take a state administered examination.

A few days later at an afternoon cocktail party, Shannon Smith, who was a member of the Rev. Michael Boss's congregation and a good friend of the priest, singled him out to talk about the murder investigation.

Shannon felt especially close to Boss because he had personally made most of the burial arrangements when the youngest of her four sons was killed in an accident.

"Don't be so sure Stanford is innocent because he passed a test in his lawyer's office," Boss warned.

When Shannon asked if Stanford had confessed to the murder, the priest became silent.

He changed the subject and soon afterwards moved away to mingle with the crowd.

Chapter 12

Obsession With Murder

Shannon Smith became friends with Frances Bemis as a result of Frances' fascination with the news coverage following Athalia's murder. Ever since the night she had walked up the street and seen her neighbor's desecrated body, Frances had been like a woman obsessed. She could hardly think or talk of much else.

She had called Shannon two days following the murder to comment on her detailed story in the *Florida Times-Union* about Athalia's background. The story mentioned Athalia's five visits to the St. Johns County Commission, specifically to complain about County Manager Stanford.

It also was after that particular story appeared on January 26, 1974, that Shannon began receiving other calls from a person or persons who would hang up a few seconds after she answered the telephone. The calls continued for about six weeks after the murder, both at Shannon's office and at home. It was never determined who made the calls because, although the calls made her uneasy enough to report them to Garrett, she had declined his offer to have a tap put on her phone.

Long before Frances and Shannon met formally at a luncheon arranged by a mutual friend, Stanley Osborne, Frances began calling Shannon at her office daily to discuss new developments in the case and to pass along the latest rumors. She said it was important for Shannon to know every speck of speculation and gossip as well as the facts because it was all grist for the mill that would eventually grind out the truth.

Stanley, who rented a cottage from Frances behind the Maria Sanchez Apartment House, told Shannon that Frances was so emotionally entrenched in the murder case that it frightened him. She reveled in sparking "who done it" debates wherever she went, particularly at cocktail parties. She kept hoping that after a few drinks someone with inside information about the Lindsley murder or the suspects would spill a prize tidbit.

Stanley was 81-years-old and a retired lecturer from Australia. But, because he liked to stay busy, he worked several nights a week as clerk at Broudy's package store. When he wasn't working, Frances included him in her social activities although there was never a spark of romance between them.

Frances had been best friends with Stanley's deceased wife, Rachael. After her death, Frances had taken it upon herself to look after Stanley, treating him as family.

After Osborne sold his home and moved into the cottage behind Frances' apartment house, the two had become closer than ever. At least once a day they had coffee and chewed the fat. Now, as Stanley told Shannon, their discussions centered around Athalia's death and for the first time ever they were beginning to have arguments. One thing they argued about was Frances' nightly walks. In view of what had happened to Athalia, Stanley considered it dangerous for Frances to walk alone. But, Frances not only continued walking, she was returning home later and later, spending more and more time, stopping off to visit with people who lived along the walk route, pumping them for information or gossip relative to Athalia's murder.

Osborne said one of the neighbors had told him Frances was behaving like a female "Columbo," and was giving the impression that she knew who killed Athalia.

"I told her to ease up. This murder is a touchy subject. Of course the poor dear doesn't know who killed Mrs. Lindsley anymore than I do. She just has an opinion like almost everyone else but she could be putting herself in danger by talking so freely about it," Stanley said. "I told her I don't want to come home some night and find her dead but of course she just laughed. She is more stubborn than a team of mules."

Stanley had passed on his concerns to Shannon after inviting her to join Frances and him for lunch on a Sunday during the heat of the murder investigation. Stanley warned Shannon that Frances would pick her like a chicken about the investigation, but, he said he was sure the two women would "get on." They had many things in common other than an interest in the murder.

Mostly to please Stanley, Shannon accepted the invitation which included cocktails at Frances' apartment before lunching at the Ponce de Leon Motor Lodge.

Shannon was en route to Maria Sanchez Apartment House when it started to pour rain. Frances was waiting on the front porch with an umbrella when the reporter pulled into the parking area fronting the house.

Frances made no effort to hide how excited she was about the "get together."

She had set out a plate of crackers and silver bowls filled with nuts, chips and two seafood dips on the antique marble-topped coffee table in her living room and then mixed drinks to order . . . serving them on a silver tray. It amused Osborne that she had put out real linen cocktail napkins he'd never seen her use before. A splash of unnecessary show, indicative of her mood that day.

The conversation began casually with talk about Osborne's former lecture circuit and then with Frances steering, moved quickly to Athalia Lindsley's murder.

Shannon sat on the chintz-covered sofa and Frances sat on the edge of an arm chair to her right, listening intently to everything the reporter said.

Frances' face was lit in a smile, the kind that made slits of her dark Oriental eyes. The slanted eyes were the only feature she had inherited from a father whom she never discussed except to say that he had been a doctor and that her mother had divorced him when Frances was very young.

There was a shade tree story that Frances' father had never practiced medicine but had been a cook in a

Chinese Restaurant in St. Augustine at the time he had married her mother. Osborne didn't believe the gossip. Frances had no reason to lie, he said.

Frances had a sallow complexion, not much improved by two daubs of orange rouge. Her reddish hair was thin, short, and colored from a bottle. She had a dumpy, shapeless figure and severe foot problems that necessitated that she wear prescription oxfords even for dress.

Although she was physically unattractive, there was a rare kind of sparkle and mysterious appeal about her. There was no mistaking that she enjoyed people. And, she had the rare gift of being a truly good listener.

She was intrigued that Shannon had been one of three people with whom Athalia had dined at her last meal.

"I'm glad you liked her. So many didn't," she said. "Athalia stood on her convictions. I especially liked that about her."

She went on to say that James Lindsley was "something of a clod--completely insensitive to people like Athalia. Their marriage had been a mistake."

"But," she had reflected, daintily reaching for a peanut, "Jim did not kill her. That murder was not his style."

Apparently, she had not expected a response. She chewed the nut pensively, stood up, lifted her glass, and took a final swallow.

"Perhaps," she said, "Unless someone cares for another drink--we should be going to lunch."

Chapter 13

County Manager Arrested

As the murder probe entered its third week, Garrett decided to offer a $500 reward to anyone turning in a weapon or other evidence that could lead to the arrest of the killer of Athalia Ponsell Lindsley.

He passed the word to reporters on St. Valentine's day after making arrangements to run a sizeable ad in the *St. Augustine Record's* weekend edition.

Specifically, what he hoped the reward might produce was a machete and clothes the killer wore during the attack. At that point, he had few if any doubts the murder weapon was a machete. If Locke McCormick's description of the killer was correct, the clothes Garrett was looking for included a white dress shirt and a pair of dark (navy blue or black) trousers. During the attack, blood had spurted and splattered and streamed in all directions. Garrett doubted that the killer could have avoided getting blood on his shirt and pants--maybe even his shoes, necessitating that he dispose of the blood stained items along with the weapon as quickly as possible after leaving the scene. If by any chance, the killer had been observed disposing of the evidence, Garrett hoped the reward money would smoke out the witness.

Garrett left reporters with the impression that the weapon and clothes were all he needed to wrap up the murder investigation and make an arrest.

The morning after he announced the reward offer, the sheriff went out of town rather mysteriously. His departure exasperated the media because he was not expected back until the following Thursday and he had not authorized anyone, in his absence, to release information on possible responses to the reward offer. His reason for leaving at that particular time was never really explained either at the time he left or after he returned.

While reporters pouted over the temporary news drought, others following the investigation were playing a guessing game.

Why, if police with all of their available tools of discovery had failed to find the murder weapon, did Garrett believe an ordinary citizen could dig it up?

Was Garrett the victim of a conniving witness who wanted to be paid for information?

Was he stalling for time because he had failed to bring in the killer?

Or, was he setting the stage to frame someone in a last ditch effort to solve the case?

Meantime, on the afternoon before Garrett returned, Jim Lindsley had gone to Athalia's house to transplant one of the young peach trees, she had recently set out, to his own yard. While he was there, two sheriff's deputies drove up, got out of the squad car and began removing a section from the iron railing around the front porch of the house.

Jim had come around the house from the back yard and was about to question their authority to do whatever they were doing when he remembered that the sheriff had called his attention to a nick in the rail the day after the murder. Garrett thought the nick probably was made by the machete during the attack on Athalia. Jim had immediately agreed to Garrett's request for permission to remove the rail section if and when he found the murder weapon.

One of the officers noticed Jim and grinned sheepishly. "Sorry, Mr. Lindsley, we didn't know you were here. The sheriff said you wouldn't mind if we did this."

"Hell no, but I hope this means that Garrett has found the machete that SOB used on my poor wife."

"Sorry. We understand your concern but we can't answer that," the officer replied.

Jim turned then and walked around the corner of the house where Locke McCormick had seen Athalia's killer disappear the evening of her murder.

When he reached the back yard, he stopped and stared angrily at the kitchen window of the Stanford home. When Athalia was alive, Lindsley had often seen Stanford peering from the window when he and Athalia were outside together. Thinking about it gave Lindsley a creepy feeling.

"Bastard," he muttered under his breath, as he carefully loaded the peach tree into the back of his station wagon. Peach trees are not indigenous to Florida and few are grown commercially in the state but Athalia had found a variety, much smaller than the commercial type peaches grown in the clay hills of Georgia, but suitable for cooking.

After driving home and carefully replanting the tree in a hole filled with dried cow manure and compost, Lindsley went inside and tried to reach Garrett, but the dispatcher at the sheriff's office said he was still out of town. When Shannon Smith ran into Jim later that day, he told her about the rail being removed from Athalia's porch. "I think it's a good sign. Someone must have turned in a machete."

Time dragged by until Garrett returned to the department on Thursday, but even then he was not ready to talk to reporters. Mila, his secretary at his courthouse office, explained that he had a morning conference with one of his investigators and would not be available until after 1:00 p.m.

Four members of the local news media were camped in the hallway outside the sheriff's department when Garrett came down the second floor corridor from the elevator a few minutes after two o'clock. Garrett's mouth spread into a wide, friendly grin, the kind people reserve for their best buddies.

"Come on in," he said, unlocking the hallway door to his office. Once inside, he opened another door and called to his secretary. "I'm back. Please hold my calls a few minutes."

He took a seat in the swivel chair behind his desk, removed a wrapper from a cigar that protruded from the pocket of his tweed sports coat, and accepted a light from a Ronson proffered by Pat Lynn.

"Okay folks," he said finally. "I know you are chomping at the bit for news but there is nothing I can tell you at this time."

A shocked hush fell over the room, followed by a cacophony of protests. A radio newscaster reminded Garrett that reporters had been waiting a week to hear about the response to the reward offer.

"I know . . . I know. But, I must ask you to be patient for another day or so. I promise all of you will be called when I have something you can print. You are welcome to some coffee before you go," Garrett grinned.

The following afternoon, exactly one week after he had announced the reward offer, Garrett went to the office of County Judge Charles Mathis to pick up a warrant the judge had signed authorizing the arrest of the man who was to be charged with the savage slaying of Athalia Ponsell Lindsley.

It was a little past 5:30, about the same time of day that Athalia had arrived home on the afternoon of her rendezvous with death a month earlier, when an unmarked sheriff's car pulled up at the curb outside the front gate at 126 Marine Street, the home of County Manager Alan Stanford.

The neighborhood was as void of signs of life as a funeral home at midnight when Garrett, Police Sgt. Dominic Nicklo and an agent for the Florida Department of Law Enforcement stepped from the car. Nothing stirred. Not even a leaf on the canopy of trees that shaded Stanford's front yard.

The three men would have welcomed the whimpering of a dog or the chattering of an angry bluejay as they stood for a moment silently questioning the awesome tranquility. None of them were comfortable about what they had to do. Athalia's vacant house stood within the range of their vision like an unfriendly ghost, reminding them of their duty.

Finally, Garrett opened the gate and the three men walked together across the yard to the front porch of the Stanford home and rang the doorbell. The bell broke the eerie silence but there was no response. Garrett had opted not to disrupt the work schedule at the county road department by arresting Stanford earlier in the day at his office. Now, as he rang the bell a second time without getting a response, he wondered if he had erred in his judgment.

"Maybe, he's out back," Nicklo said, sensing Garrett's anxiety.

"Yeah . . . let's go see," Garrett nodded and led the way around the house, where the officers found Alan and Patti Stanford sitting just outside the back porch watching their three-year-old daughter playing with her dolls near a swing set.

Apparently, the Stanfords had not heard the bell. Patti looked up in surprise at the officers. Alan stood up to acknowledge their presence, his face void of expression. He was still wearing the dress shirt and dark trousers he had worn to work that day. He had not even loosened his blue and white striped tie. Garrett guessed the family might have been planning to go out to dinner, unaware of what was coming. He had told only one person in the department about getting the warrant. To his knowledge

Nicklo had told no one except his chief. Apparently, for once, there had been no leaks.

The child continued to play, oblivious to the arrival of visitors. Garrett didn't want her upset so he went over to Stanford to warn him in a whisper of the impending arrest. It was made in the kitchen with Garrett reading the warrant and Nicklo reading Stanford his rights. Mrs. Stanford had remained outdoors with their young daughter, Annette.

Through it all Stanford said nothing. Not a hair of emotion crossed his face. No surprise, no hurt, no anger. When he finally spoke, he asked to call his attorney. Within an hour, Stanford was taken to the courthouse for a first appearance before Judge Mathis and then on to the St. Johns County Jail where he was held until his arraignment the following Tuesday.

St. Augustine's two radio stations led the parade in breaking the news of Stanford's arrest with late night bulletins informing listeners that the county manager was being held without bond in the county jail, charged with the brutal slaying of his next door neighbor, Athalia Ponsell Lindsley.

Details were skimpy. Newsmen said Garrett, who had commandeered the investigation and made the arrest, would not divulge the nature of the evidence he had amassed that linked Stanford to the grisly crime.

The sheriff had refused to comment on a report that someone, baited by a promise of a $500 reward, had turned in a bloodstained machete and a bag of bloody clothes.

Jacksonville television stations featured the arrest story as the first spot on the eleven o'clock evening news.

Anchors said details of what prompted the arrest of the prominent county official were not available at deadline.

The Saturday morning edition of the *Florida Times-Union* played the story in an eight-column spread with a banner headline across the top of the front page. The story implied that Garrett's $500 reward offer may have paid off. But, the sheriff would not confirm a report that someone had found the evidence he needed to wrap up the case.

Garrett was quoted as saying that it would not be proper for him to discuss the kind of evidence that led to Stanford's arrest because he expected to be called as a witness when the case got to court. The intimation was he had solved the mystery but the suspense would continue until the trial.

The story mentioned that Stanford had engaged the services of a local attorney the day after the murder but that the attorney could not be reached to comment on an unconfirmed report that Stanford also had retained a Jacksonville criminal lawyer to assist with his defense. The paper's coverage included a sidebar story that described Stanford as "a quiet, serious-mannered man who was unanimously picked by the St. Johns County Commission two years earlier to step into the role of county manager and road superintendent."

The story noted his membership on the Trinity Parish vestry and quoted friends as saying he was a devoted husband and father to his wife and three daughters. The *St. Augustine Record's* Saturday account of the arrest offered no pertinent new information, but the writer tried to freshen the account with a touch of melodrama.

He began the saga, saying "four weeks of anxiety and rumor in the wake of the slaying of Mrs. Athalia Ponsell Lindsley ended last night, quietly and without drama."

"The 49-year-old county manager, known for his quiet demeanor and self control, betrayed no emotion when he was arrested at his home."

During his first few hours in jail Stanford had two visitors: his wife and a reporter from the *Record*. He had refused to speak with the reporter. The county manager was in no mood to answer questions. Besides, his attorney had advised against it.

The *Record* story gave mini profiles of both Stanford and the man who had stalked him since the day after his neighbor's murder. The story said "the murder of Mrs. Athalia Ponsell Lindsley became something of an obsession with Garrett. He became personally involved from the night of Jan. 23 . . . in the following weeks, he pushed much of his administrative workload aside or assigned it to secretaries and deputies as he doggedly pursued the murder case."

"*Record* reporters frequently saw him late at night as he made his way from the sheriff's office to parts unknown in his unmarked car . . . One time, during the wee hours of morning, a reporter interviewed Garrett at the county jail around 1:30 a.m. . . . when the reporter called the sheriff's office at 8:00 a.m. that morning for additional information, the sheriff's was already at work."

The story described both Stanford and Garrett as "low-key individuals." The two men share much in common. Both are quiet, soft-spoken, more eager to discuss than debate. Neither is given to extravagant motion nor speech. Both men prefer to listen rather than talk, to read faces, accept well-meaning advice and handle people with deference.

"Last night, those two personalities quietly clashed. Typical of both men, it was done coolly, without fanfare or drama."

Garrett was surprised and disappointed by some of the reaction to Stanford's arrest. His phone was ringing when Garrett arrived at the office the next morning. A husky-voiced woman, who refused to give her name, began railing at him, using gutter language to express her outrage over "Alan's arrest." She accused Garrett of framing the county manager to avoid being stuck with "another unsolved murder."

"You are a no good, lazy, son of a bitch. I'm going to do everything in my power to see that you are never re-elected," the woman had said before hanging up.

Then, Garrett's secretary buzzed to say Herbie Wiles, the chairman of the county commission, was waiting on another line.

Before picking up the phone, Garrett fortified himself with a large gulp of black coffee from the cup his secretary had just set in front of him. The chairman was brief and to the point. "I've never questioned any of your decisions before, Dudley. But, I really believe you have made a mistake. It could backfire, you know. Right now, a lot of people feel that Alan is the hero and you are the villain."

Garrett sighed, and finished off the coffee.

There also were supportive calls that morning from people like James Lindsley and Frances Bemis who wanted to offer their congratulations. "I'd like to kill the

SOB myself and save the state the expense of a trial," Lindsley barked.

"Now, hold on there Jinx, I don't want to have to bring YOU in for murder," Garrett joshed.

That morning Shannon Smith received a call from Jean Troemel who said she was reading the story of Alan's arrest in the morning newspaper when she was distracted by "a lot of racket in the front yard." "You know me--I had to go to see what was going on. Guess what . . . that tree over there by my (artist) studio was full of bluejays. There were a staggering number of birds--all screaming at once. I seldom ever see more than one jay at a time in the yard. The birds reminded me of Clementine, Athalia's jay, and all the other injured birds she befriended. The more I listened to the noise the birds were making, the more I believed they were out there screaming the news that their friend's killer had been caught," Mrs. Troemel said.

"This case is riddled with bluejays," Shannon said. "I guess Frances will make something of it."

Indeed, Frances Bemis was fascinated by the bird story.

"When birds congregate like that, it means something," she told Jean. "In this case, I believe it is a good omen. I think it means Garrett has scored, got the right man," she said. "Why don't you get your camera and take a picture--or better still you could paint them." But, when Jean returned to the window, the jays had disappeared as mysteriously as they appeared.

Chapter 14

Accused and Jobless

When she was alive, Athalia had been unsuccessful in all of her efforts to get Alan Stanford removed from his prestigious post. But, in death, she was finally going to have her way.

Three days after Stanford's arrest, the five county commissioners gathered in a special session that lasted less than 30 minutes. The emergency meeting was called for the sole purpose of granting Mr. Stanford an indefinite leave of absence.

It was a quickly organized move on the part of the commissioners who were walking on eggshells.

Stanford was due to be arraigned in county court the following day. Though many judges refuse to set bond for people charged with heinous crimes, commissioners were aware there was political pressure on Judge Charles Mathis to grant an exception in the case of Alan Stanford.

If Mathis set bond, that meant Stanford would expect to return to his job at the county road department while awaiting trial, and that possibility was posing problems. Some valuable county employees already were balking at the idea of having to work for a man accused of murder.

Two board members favored asking for Stanford's resignation but that would place commissioners in a position of condemning him ahead of a jury. At least one commissioner believed Garrett had arrested the wrong candidate. Even before Stanford was arrested Herbie Wiles had stated publicly that he did not believe Alan Stanford was capable of such a vicious act as Athalia's murder. He opened the special commission meeting with a prayer for the accused official.

Aside from Wiles' personal convictions, there was more public sympathy for Stanford than three of the commissioners, who planned to seek re-election that year, could afford to ignore. It was in the best interest of their political futures that they present an image of "fairness" in dealing with the touchy situation.

The morning after Stanford was charged in the murder, Willard Howatt, the attorney for the county commission, asked for a conference with Stanford's attorney, Frank Upchurch, Jr., and advised him of the alternatives open to Stanford. He could either request a leave of absence or face the possibility of termination, meaning he would have no job to return to if he were acquitted. Howatt also advised Upchurch that if the leave were granted, the county was not obligated to continue paying Stanford's salary. Commissioners were the stewards of taxpayers' money. Paying him to stay home was not advisable. Howatt also was concerned that granting a leave of absence with pay might be construed as an indirect contribution to Stanford's defense.

Stanford had been furious when he heard his alternatives. He did not want a leave of absence. He wanted a job waiting for him if he were acquitted.

But, after considerable argument with his attorney, Stanford composed the following letter which Chairman Wiles read aloud at the special meeting:

"I have been arrested and charged with a serious crime, a crime I assure you I did not commit. While I can ill afford the loss of income at this time, I do not feel that I could expect to continue my duties while I stand accused."

"Therefore, I request that I be granted a leave of absence for an indefinite period of time until final disposition of the pending charges."

Commissioners unanimously approved the request and then appointed Pete Hardeman to fill the slot of acting county manager.

Hardeman was the road and bridge department supervisor and a logical choice because he had served as acting manager once before in the interim between the resignation of County Engineer Gordon Hayes and the hiring of Stanford.

But, the choice must have blistered Stanford's pride. Hardeman was the first man Stanford had attempted to fire shortly after he took over duties as county manager in January of 1972.

Stanford had given Hardeman the axe without consulting the commission, but because Hardeman was a long and faithful employee, the board had called in both men for a confrontation at a public meeting.

County road department employees had packed commission chambers to protest the firing of Hardeman.

Commissioners had permitted Stanford to speak first.

Flushed and obviously irritated at spotting so many road and bridge people among the spectators, Stanford began to explain why it had been necessary to fire the popular, longtime employee. Stanford alleged that since his first day on the job Hardeman had been trying to undermine his authority.

"He won't follow orders and he is confusing the other workers and causing a great deal of friction . . . "

Stanford hesitated because of the commotion in the room. Some of the employees had started to boo him and one was yelling "he's a liar."

Dan Mickler, the then chairman of the commission, reached for his gavel, demanding order.

Stanford then alleged that Hardeman was maneuvering "to turn all of the employees against me." "I'd like to know who excused these men from work today," Stanford asked the commission.

The booing had started again and Mickler, cracking the gavel, ruled that the employees had a right to be present at the hearing but "all of you will have to leave if these interruptions continue."

When Hardeman spoke, he agreed there had been dissension in the department, but he said he had done nothing to trigger it. He blamed the entire problem on Stanford.

"He has a bad temper and he simply doesn't know how to get along with the men. Some of them have had a lot more experience in road work than he has, but he refuses to listen to advice or delegate any authority."

Hardeman blamed Stanford for a sizeable turnover in road and bridge department workers since Stanford had taken over.

There was a loud burst of applause from employees as Hardeman concluded that "the situation is going to get worse."

The stormy session ended with the board voting 3-2 to overrule the county manager and restore Hardeman to his job as supervisor of road and bridge work.

"I hope we've heard the end of this. It appears to me it is nothing more than a personality conflict," Mickler commented.

"We expect the two of you to settle your differences like gentlemen," Mickler added, addressing Stanford and Hardeman.

After appointing Hardeman to take over for Stanford while he awaited trial, commissioners set his salary at $1,000 a month, considerably less than the $20,000 yearly salary commissioners had recently approved for Stanford.

The same morning Hardeman took over Stanford's duties, the prisoner was removed from his private cell at the county jail and driven downtown to the courthouse in a maximum security van for an arraignment before County Judge Charles Mathis.

Spectators began gathering in the hallway half an hour before a court bailiff unlocked the double doors to the third floor courtroom.

A number of friends of the Stanford family were milling around near the elevator when the door opened and Mrs. Stanford stepped out, accompanied by her daughter, Patricia, and the Rev. Michael Boss.

Mrs. Stanford was powdered, perfumed, and fashionably dressed in an expensive looking navy blue suit. She gushed through the crowd, beaming like a celebrity on opening night, nodding to friends and squeezing out-stretched hands.

She smiled and waved to reporters and a television cameraman who had clustered just outside the entrance to the courtroom.

Still smiling, Mrs. Stanford entered the courtroom, blew a kiss to a woman who was already seated on a back row, and walked swiftly to a front bench on the same side of the room where her husband would sit with his attorneys.

Once she had settled herself between the Rev. Boss and her daughter, she opened her purse, took out a stick of gum, removed the wrapper and popped the gum into her mouth, chewing furiously while she waited for court to convene.

Once or twice, she glanced over her shoulder, checking out faces among the spectators who had squeezed together into every available inch of bench space, like churchgoers on Easter Sunday.

Noise drifted from the hallway--voices of people who had arrived too late to find a seat. A bailiff was refusing to allow them to stand inside.

Finally, Stanford appeared, entering from the side doorway near the judge's bench. A sheriff's deputy ha removed his handcuffs and stood in the doorway whil Stanford walked to the table where his attorney already was seated.

Stanford was wearing a tan business suit. He looked relaxed, not at all like a man who had been locked up for the first time in his life and accused of a crime that could send him to the electric chair if he were convicted.

He turned and gave his family members and the minister sitting in the front row a warm smile. Then his eyes swept across the courtroom and he beamed as though pleased at the turnout.

Later, standing before the judge, listening to Assistant State Attorney Richard Watson read the formal charge against him, Stanford folded his arms, assuming the air of a member of a debating team, tolerantly giving the floor to an opponent.

"The state charges you with unlawfully killing Athalia Ponsell Lindsley on January 23 with a knife, commonly known as a machete," Watson said.

"How do you plead?" Judge Mathis' voice was unusually stern.

"My client enters a plea of not guilty, your honor," Stanford's attorney, Frank Upchurch, responded.

There followed a brief debate over whether Stanford should be released on bond. Judge Mathis looked displeased, saying, "I'm not inclined to set bond on a charge of this nature." Upchurch argued there was no justification for holding Alan Stanford without bond because "he has no reason to flee. He has been a prime suspect in this thing since the beginning and has made no attempt to leave town. He has been cooperative and responsive to any request I've made. I assure you he will remain here with his family. He is well liked in the community and his friends have offered to post bond."

Watson said the state was opposed to bail "in this particular case." But, should Mathis decide to set bond, Watson requested that it not be less than $100,000. After a period of silent deliberation, Mathis, in a near whisper, set the bond at $20,000.

James Lindsley, who was stowed away on a back bench of the courtroom, was gnashing his teeth like someone having a bad dream.

Chapter 15

Reporters Get A Story

Stanford was in good spirits as he rode back to the jail from the hearing. His attorney had assured him that his bond would be posted that afternoon and he should be out of jail and home by supper time.

He was relieved at the low amount of bail particularly since more than one attorney had warned him that it was customary for judges to require bonds of $100,000 for persons charged with first degree murder. Raising that kind of bail money could have taken days, maybe weeks. He already was facing a financial bind due to losing his salary.

He also was relieved that Walter Arnold, an attorney who was considered to be the cream of North Florida's crop of criminal defense wizards, had agreed to defend him.

For once, he did not feel threatened by the ring of reporters he saw waiting for him in the jail parking lot when he stepped from the van. He had been so angered and hurt by some of the press stories before his arrest that in one of his more hostile moments he had rudely rejected an interview with a feature writer from an out of town newspaper, saying, "I shouldn't even tell you my middle name." Now, perhaps the time had come for him to use the newspaper pests to help set the record straight.

"If they want an interview, let's do it outside," he whispered to Deputy Charles Cannon. Stanford dreaded going back to his cell even for a few hours.

Lt. Cannon, who was then chief officer at the county jail, but was later shot to death in a domestic squabble, had personally driven the prisoner to the court-house and back that morning. Cannon got along well with most of the local reporters. In fact, it was Cannon who had passed the word along the press grapevine that a county employee had turned in the evidence Garrett needed "to nail Stanford."

Cannon had no personal love for the county manager. He partially blamed Stanford for the rundown physical state at the county jail. He and Stanford had numerous arguments over what needed to be done in the way of remodeling and repairs. Cannon really didn't care if the press crucified Stanford. Cannon was scheduled to go home for lunch but, rather than call a relief officer, he stayed to hear what his prisoner had to say.

It was a 75-degree day but Stanford looked cool as a refrigerated cucumber, as he began responding to questions.

He began by saying, "there's been a terrible mistake . . . I am totally innocent of this thing."

"How can you be so calm?" The question came from Patrick Lynn.

Stanford smiled. "Do I look that cool? I put a lot of trust in the Lord."

He said he had no idea what kind of evidence Garrett was holding against him, "but, I am not guilty," he said, explaining that at the time his neighbor was killed, "I was in that office right there."

He pointed to a white shingled house adjacent to the jail and then went on to say that "I have witnesses who can corroborate I was at the office at the time." He declined to name the witnesses, saying only that there were five people willing to testify for him at the trial.

Stanford patiently retraced his movements on the evening of the murder. He had come home from work at 5:15, changed clothes and then returned to the office ten or fifteen minutes before six o'clock.

"I wanted to make sure some permits we had worked on for months had been mailed out correctly." The county needed the permits to build an artificial fishing reef and "there might have been some errors." As it turned out, everything was in order, but he had stayed on 40 minutes or so to study an engineering text.

Someone asked Stanford what he knew about a machete and a bag of bloody clothes the sheriff was holding as evidence.

"I've heard about that. But, I don't know anything about a machete and clothes. They aren't mine." Stanford tilted his chin defensively and glared at Lt. Cannon, who was leaning against the jail van, covering his mouth to stifle a yawn, or, more likely, a smile.

Stanford was aware that Cannon did not believe he was innocent and he suspected that the chief jailer had been bad mouthing him to the press.

Now, Cannon had lowered his eyes and was pushing a piece of gravel around in the parking lot with the polished toe of one of his size 13 shoes as Stanford began denying ever having had any arguments with Athalia Ponsell Lindsley. "We had practically no communication across the fence during the two years we lived side by side. I guess I talked to her less than five times."

What did he think about Watson's proposal to move the trial to another county? Someone changed the subject.

Stanford was opposed to the idea, regardless of all the publicity generated by the murder.

"I would prefer to be tried right here," he said, adding that he had faith that "the people of St. Johns County are reasonable and would give me a fair trial."

"He's lying. Everyone in this neighborhood knows better." Frances Bemis was sipping a gin and tonic and tearing apart statements Stanford had made in a story published on the front page of the *St. Augustine Record* on Tuesday, February 26.

Frances had invited Katherine Hawkins, Helen Strong, a published author of a book called a *Pig in a Poke*, and Shannon Smith for cocktails.

"It is ridiculous that he would deny all the fights he had with Athalia," she complained.

"The problem is Athalia is dead. She can't come back to dispute anything he says. Who else actually heard them fighting?" Shannon asked.

"His wife, and, probably the McCormicks. Rosemary had a few arguments with Athalia herself. She and Patti Stanford talked all the time. And, they even took her to court. Don't tell me he wasn't involved in that," Frances shot back.

"So, what can you do about it? What he says won't matter if Garrett has the evidence they say he has," Helen Strong broke in. "Relax and drink your drink."

"What do you think he has?" Frances directed the question to Shannon.

"If what I heard is true, he has plenty. Someone told me there was a watch, a pair of shoes and even a couple of blood stained baby diapers in the bag of clothes that was found in the swamp . . . The diapers supposedly were used as rags after little Annette was toilet trained."

"Let's hope what you heard is right, my dear," Frances replied, reaching for Helen's empty glass.

"Another highball, Helen?"

"I guess so . . . but let me tell you something that is worrying me sick."

Everyone stared at her. Helen Strong was no gossip.

"What now?" Shannon asked.

"Well, it's my understanding that our church is going to start a collection for Alan's defense. I personally think we should try and stop it."

"You mean Trinity Episcopal?" Shannon asked.

Helen nodded. "Yes--our church. I think you should call Boss and give him Hell."

"Well, he was in court today. I can understand he has to stand by the family," Shannon said.

Helen made a strange noise in her throat. "Standing by is one thing. Collecting money is something else. I don't like it one bit."

Frances had returned from the kitchen with fresh drinks. "What does James Lindsley have to say about all this, Shannon? You keep in touch."

"I had lunch with him after the hearing and he was so mad about the $20,000 bond he couldn't eat, took his lunch home in a doggy bag," the reporter replied.

"I can't say that I blame him. That $20,000 bond is a joke," Frances said. "What do you think, Katherine? You haven't said a word. Are you bored?" Frances asked.

"Bored? You've got to be kidding." Katherine, a heavy smoker, responded in a voice coarse as gravel. "There hasn't been anything as exciting as this murder in years. You know I didn't know Mrs. Lindsley and I don't know anything about Mr. Stanford. If the sheriff thinks he's guilty, that's good enough for me no matter what this fellow says to the newspapers. As you know, I voted for Garrett. He's not going to hang an innocent man."

Chapter 16

Grand Jury
Sees Evidence

The sky was black with storm clouds the morning of February 28 when a Grand Jury panel went behind closed doors at 9:00 a.m. to examine the evidence in the state's case against Alan Stanford.

The accused sat in the living room of his Marine Street home, trying to concentrate on reading a book but it was wasted effort.

Stanford was not superstitious. He didn't look for warnings the way his neighbor, Athalia, had done. He told himself the weather had no bearing on any decision the Grand Jury would reach that day or the next, however long it took for state attorneys to question their witnesses.

Stanford kept reminding himself how lucky he was to be out of jail. Those three nights locked up in a dingy cell were more depressing than he had ever imagined. For sure, the St. Johns County Jail was not the nation's finest.

It was in sore need of a face lift and all kinds of improvements.

Lt. Cannon had been complaining to him about the jail for months before the murder of Stanford's incorrigible neighbor. He had chosen to ignore Cannon's request that he inspect the jail and make recommendations to county commissioners for improvements.

When Stanford had complained to Cannon about the tiny light bulb in his cell, Cannon had shrugged. "We don't have color TV, silk sheets, or 100-watt bulbs." Stanford hated Cannon's sarcasm, but what the hell? Stanford regarded him as one of Sheriff Garrett's "incompetent henchmen." Stanford only hoped to God he would never have to go back there or to any other prison. His attorneys had assured him the grand jury review was just a formality. The state attorney needed the panel to give its seal of approval to the evidence Garrett had collected before taking the case to trial. There was a hair of a chance the grand jury would decide the evidence was too flimsy and hand in a "no true" bill but the odds were poor that would happen.

Upchurch, his local attorney, had explained that the state holds the upper hand in a grand jury probe. Jurors don't hear anything prosecutors don't want them to know. No matter what prosecutors show or tell them, there is no defense attorney around to object. No one to testify to the innocence of the accused. In other words "it's a stacked deck," Stanford thought miserably.

Not to worry, Upchurch had said. Even if the grand jury indicted him, an indictment is not a conviction. It did not prove his guilt. It merely gave the state a green light to begin preparing for a jury trial. That was supposed to be a comfort even though it meant spending thousands of dollars in lawyers' fees in the hope of convincing a trial jury he was innocent.

The nature of a grand jury probe is never divulged until after the panel has decided whether or not to indict. But, Stanford and everyone else from the courthouse janitor to Circuit Judge Howell Melton knew that the murder of Athalia Ponsell Lindsley was to be the subject of the February 28 probe.

Stanford was pleased that the session was closed to reporters in addition to the general public. Even if reporters were called as witnesses--and Stanford had heard that those reporters who regularly covered county commission meetings had been subpoenaed to testify--they would have to swear not to write a word about what they said or saw or heard in the jury room. The "jerks" would be limited to reporting only names of people they observed going in and out of the hearing room. They were also barred from talking to any of the witnesses.

Minutes after 9:00 a.m., police officers walked briskly down the hallway that led to the third floor jury room, carrying large brown paper bags, that presumably shrouded the murder weapon, and other important pieces of evidence. Five professional-looking men and women, carrying brief cases and small bags and boxes, followed and were offered seats in a tiny office across from the jury room where Capt. R.W. Williams was standing by to put in calls to other witnesses, as needed.

State Attorney Stephen Boyles was expecting a marathon session and did not want all the witnesses called in at one time. Boyles didn't want any of 20 witnesses consulting with one another or, worse yet, getting button-holed by a reporter.

The day crawled.

"I feel as though I've been sitting in a doctor's office all day," James Lindsley grumbled after he was finally called to testify as the last witness of the day.

Shortly after 5:00 p.m., Boyles opened the door, looking bushed, and told Williams that the panel had recessed until 9:00 a.m. Friday morning. "Watson has to go jog. The rest of us go home and drink at five o'clock." Boyles joked.

After Boyles left, eighteen jurors, somber as pallbearers, followed the foreman, Dr. William J. McClure, the head of Florida's School for the Deaf and the Blind, out the door and down the hallway to the elevators. Watson came into the hallway and stood like a watch dog to be sure one of three reporters still hanging around didn't try to talk to one of them.

It was about 4:30 the following afternoon when Joe Mosely, the grand jury court reporter, carried his paraphernalia into the hallway and sat down in a chair by the window to wait while the grand jury began secret deliberations.

At five o'clock, the courtroom was already crowded with spectators, mostly court house employees who had heard the panel might be coming in.

County Commissioner Richard Parks was seated with one of the custodians on the third row behind a delegation of local reporters.

He was talking in a rather loud voice to the custodian, defending his position in having voted with the board to hire Stanford.

"I knew it was a mistake. I wanted to hire an engineer. But, I was the only one who didn't want him but I went along because I didn't think it looked good for a man to be hired in a split vote."

At one point, Parks leaned over and began talking privately to Shannon Smith who was seated directly in front of him.

"I'll bet you good money he ain't going to be indicted. I say they'll have to let him off because the sheriff's got no evidence."

"You know that for a fact?" Shannon asked.

"Well, the sheriff hasn't said so if he has. Only thing that worries me is that I heard they've got a watch with blood on it that somebody found and a jeweler has identified it as the one he repaired for Stanford. I can't believe a jeweler would swear to a lie like that. I heard he testified before the grand jury."

"Still," Parks added, "I say they will let him off."

About that time the Rev. Michael Boss entered the courtroom and came to sit beside Shannon.

He said he had come directly from the Stanford home and that Alan and his family had elected not to be present for the grand jury presentment.

"They are expecting the worst," Boss said.

Then at exactly 5:30 in the afternoon, Judge Howell Melton took his seat on the bench and waited as the bailiff escorted the panel to the jury box.

All whispering ceased. You could have heard the drop of a paper clip.

Dr. Bill McClure, the foreman of the grand jury, handed the bill to the bailiff, who in turn, handed it to Melton.

There followed an awesome silence as Melton looked at the bill and then handed it over to Oliver Lawton, the clerk of court, who was one of Stanford's Marine Street neighbors. Lawton looked miserable as he silently read the bill. Spectators waited impatiently, watching him swallowing a lump in his throat.

Finally, Oliver looked helplessly at the judge.

"He's not going to read it?" Ivan Perry, a local radio announcer asked, tapping Shannon on the shoulder. Reporters and others in the courtroom could only assume that Stanford had been indicted when Judge Melton asked: "is the defendant in custody?"

State Attorney Boyles was on his feet immediately, explaining that Mr. Stanford was free on a $20,000 bond. Boyles said he was prepared to offer a motion to change the status of the bond.

The Rev. Boss sighed. "I guess that means he was indicted," he said to no one in particular.

Melton did not want to discuss bond at that point. There would be time for that later, he said, and without further explanation, dismissed the court.

Garrett, who had been sitting in the back row of the seats reserved for people called for jury duty, motioned to a deputy who had been standing by waiting to re-arrest Stanford."You might as well go home." He sighed.

Then, the sheriff went with reporters to the bench to read the indictment. As Garrett had hoped, the grand jury had not softened the charge. The indictment spelled out "premeditated, first degree murder."

Garrett read the pronouncement and then without comment left the courtroom and lit a cigar, standing quietly in a corner of the hallway as prosecutors emerged, heeled by frustrated reporters demanding to know why Oliver Lawton had refused to read the indictment and why Judge Melton had not immediately revoked Stanford's bond?

Boyles was not prepared to say when the state would ask to have the bond revoked. In fact, Boyles said over his shoulder as he moved swiftly along the corridor, he was not prepared to answer any other questions that day.

Chapter 17

Episcopalians Split

Anyone betting that Stanford would remain free despite the indictment was staking a winner.

Stanford had stood as immobile as a figure in a waxed museum, waiting for Attorney Upchurch to enter a not guilty plea before Judge Melton at the preliminary hearing the Monday following his indictment. Upchurch requested that the decision on the prosecutor's request to revoke bond be delayed until Stanford could be represented by his Jacksonville attorney, Walter Arnold. Melton had agreed though Upchurch said Arnold expected to be tied up with other cases for at least another two months.

Stanford left the courtroom, smiling. His attorneys had practically assured him that he would not have to face the nightmare of going back to jail before the trial. He had proven he could be trusted not to run away. In the face of such good behavior, there would be no real reason for a judge to punish him by locking him up to await trial.

For the time being, Stanford's chief concern was financial. Church friends, bless them, were collecting a fund to help offset the cost of his defense. But, without his salary from the county, it was going to be difficult for the Stanford family to meet expenses. He didn't have that much of a nest egg to fall back on. No doubt, it would have pleased Athalia that he was considering selling the family's new car, a 1974 Lincoln Continental, the kind of automobile Stanford and his wife had dreamed of owning all their married life.

"We have no choice, we have to live," he told his wife.

The Stanford daughter Annette's godfather had offered to loan Stanford a Cadillac if the Lincoln was sold. The Cadillac had some age on it but it was in good condition. It wouldn't be easy keeping up the mortgage payments on the Marine Street house but both Alan and Patti had worked so hard remodeling the middle-aged house, neither of them could bear the thought of giving it up. If his attorneys could keep Stanford out of jail, a friend had promised to use his influence to help him get a job at Desco Marine, an outfit that built and repaired shrimp boats in St. Augustine. Stanford did, after all, have a degree in marine engineering. If he landed the job, it not only would help the family, it would boost his image in the community.

Stanford was beginning to feel a little more comfortable and less resentful about the newspaper coverage of the murder investigation, so much so that he made a trip to the *St. Augustine Record* to thank the editor for the fairness with which the paper had addressed the most recent developments, his arrest and the grand jury indictment, in particular. Stanford was secretly relieved that there had been no editorials recommending or even suggesting that his bond be revoked. He wasn't annoyed or embarrassed that reporters had learned about the defense fund his church friends had started. Stanford regarded the fund as a kind of slap at Garrett and the men who would be prosecuting him for the death of his neighbor, especially Assistant State Attorney Richard Watson, who was a member of Trinity Parish Church.

Stanford thought it was an even bigger slap at Garrett when the *Florida Times-Union* reported that County Commissioner Wiles' insurance agency had contributed to the defense fund. The county commission chairman was quoted in the story as saying he also might contribute to the fund, "but it isn't anyone's business whether I do or not."

Stanford read the comment and grinned. That was telling 'em. Stanford tried not to worry about the other side to the story of the church's involvement in his defense.

Not everyone peering over the Book of Common Prayer at Sunday services approved of what was being done in support of the vestryman. Some of the members were threatening to withdraw their pledges because the rector was allowing the church office to be used to receive contributions to the defense fund. Carver Harris, a former member of the vestry and a real Garrett fan, was among the angriest of the flock. At a cocktail party one evening, Carver described Sunday service as "a side show with Stanford sitting piously on the front row and then running around afterwards shaking hands with total strangers like someone running for public office instead of a man accused of murdering his neighbor."

Harris said it made him ill to see "Poor Dudley-- finest sheriff we ever had--going around as chagrined as a guard dog that has been scolded for biting a burglar." Harris also mailed a magazine article to Shannon Smith's office that told of the reaction of a New England town to the arrest of a young man, who was accused of murdering his mother. Harris had underscored with a red pencil a line that read: "In an effort to absolve its own collective guilt, the town is pulling for the boy's acquittal." Attached to the article was a one-line note signed by Harris. The note asked: "Does this article ring a bell?"

Just as the murder had triggered a flurry of rumors and speculation, the support for Stanford activated imaginations within and outside of the church. Some people were saying that the support for Stanford was motivated by politics rather than Christian charity. The speculation was that Stanford and some of his supporters had been involved in shady political deals and supporters were afraid Stanford would sing to the state and drag them down if they didn't help him. It was all talk and never was there any proof to back it up.

One church member, Bill Daniell, who was curator for a museum in St. Augustine, joked about it all saying that "if the truth is ever uncovered about this case, it will make Watergate look like a Sunday School picnic. Half our people will have to change their address--to Raiford (a state prison in Florida)."

Some of Stanford's supporters also were saying cruel things about Athalia. Assistant State Attorney

Watson bristled when he heard they were saying it didn't really matter whether or not Athalia's killer was punished because "she deserved what she got." Watson wondered how some of the people who made the comment would feel if one of their relatives had been the one hacked to death. Watson wrote a letter to Michael Boss, demanding a list of names of Stanford supporters. He had decided to use the list to try and show it would be difficult to select a jury of totally unbiased individuals unless the trial was moved from St. Johns County.

Meantime, James Lindsley took action on his own in protest of the church fund raising and wrote a letter to Hamilton West, the bishop of the Episcopal Diocese of North Florida.

"I am outraged as are so many other people in St. Augustine--even numerous members of Trinity Episcopal Church," Lindsley wrote.

"My poor, defenseless wife was hacked to death, allegedly by this fiend. Yet, you people seem to regard him as a candidate for canonization."

"Funeral services were held at St. Johns Cathedral in Jacksonville for my beloved Athalia Ponsell Lindsley on January 28, 1974. She and her family were members of your church for years and years," the letter continued.

"But, it now appears your man at Trinity thinks it more proper to pray for the wolf than the slaughtered lamb," he said in icy conclusion.

About a month later Lindsey received a brief reply from Bishop West: "I can understand your outrage but we pray for the guilty as well as the innocent."

Lindsley cursed the Bishop and then settled down in sulky silence, impatiently waiting for the court to set a date for Stanford's trial.

Chapter 18

Prosecution Takes a Whipping

In mid-April, Stanford's Jacksonville defense counsel, Walter Arnold, tried to get the court to throw out the grand jury indictment. Motions began hatching like fertile eggs with Arnold challenging everything from the procedure the county used in making up the list of people called for jury duty to the legality of the sheriff's search of Stanford's home prior to his arrest.

Arnold left no technical stones unturned. He moved that charges against Stanford be dismissed because the news media had violated the defendant's civil rights prior to his arrest and because his possible conviction could result in the accused man being sentenced to death in Florida's electric chair. Arnold alleged that the death penalty is cruel and unusual punishment because "it is not imposed in many states" other than Florida.

A hearing on the motions was set for nine-thirty on the morning of April 29. Chief Circuit Judge E. L. Eastmoore, of Palatka, was assigned to hear them.

Although the indictment was not dismissed, prosecutors took a whipping at the hearing. The real set back for the prosection came just prior to the hearing. After filing motions for the state, Assistant State Attorney Richard Watson announced that he was resigning his post. At that time the office of assistant state attorney was considered a part-time post and the salary was $15,900 a year, a pittance for a man of Watson's abilities. Watson said his duties as prosecutor were so demanding he had little or no time left for private practice or his wife and three children. In resigning, Watson recommended that State Attorney Stephen Boyles make the post full-time and increase the pay accordingly.

Watson's decision to pull out came as a blow to Garrett who knew him to be a tough and successful prosecutor, one not easily intimidated by the legal stunts of criminal defense experts like Arnold. Watson was temporarily replaced with a retired Army officer and professor of law at St. Johns River Community College in Palatka. Before pulling out, Watson spent hours writing the two most important pre-trial motions. One was a lengthy document, listing specific reasons why prosecutors wanted the trial moved out of St. Johns County.

Following are the reasons he gave for seeking the change of venue:

1. A fair and impartial trial is impossible in St. Johns County.

2. The nature of the crime and Stanford's feud with Athalia Lindsley was given extensive coverage by newspapers and television stations. That coverage included the results of a polygraph test administered to Stanford by a private operator, to which the state was not a party.

3. Friends of Stanford have been soliciting money to pay a defense attorney and to assist in the support of the Stanford family. Because of the numerous solicitations, "a general feeling of sympathy for the defendant is being encouraged and promoted by fund raisers."

4. Prior to the grand jury indictment (of Stanford) articles appeared in the St. Augustine paper, alleging that the defendant's civil rights were violated. The articles also reported the grief and misery that the Stanford family suffered because he was a suspect.

5. Stanford and his family "have been the subject of prayers in St. Augustine churches, and the chairman of the St. Johns County Commission opened one meeting of the commission with a prayer for Stanford. There have been numerous statements by local citizens that Mrs. Lindsley deserved what she got."

6. The publicity given to the case, the position of the defendant as county manager at the time of the slaying, the public worship for Stanford and his family and the extensive press coverage of the case had engendered a widespread hostility toward the State of Florida with the

result that "it has become impractical and psychologically impossible" for the state to get a fair trial in St. Johns County.

7. "It is impractical to procure a jury which would determine the case solely on the evidence."

Watson's other motion addressed the state's reason for wanting Stanford back in jail while awaiting trial.

The motion said Stanford was charged with first-degree murder, a capital offense in Florida, and that granting bail to someone so charged was contrary to the Florida Constitution. The motion also cited the displeasure expressed by Garrett and others after Judge Mathis freed Stanford on a minimal $20,000 bond.

One of Arnold's motions had demanded that prosecutors give him a list identifying the 91 pieces of evidence the state planned to introduce when Stanford went on trial. Before leaving office, Watson prepared and filed the reply. Although it answered many of the questions Garrett had refused to answer at the time he arrested Stanford, the list did not come as a revelation to many people, especially those who kept abreast of all the rumors and arm-chair speculation.

As James Lindsley's friend, St. Augustine Beach Mayor Joe McClure was fond of saying: "Everyone I know has a magnifying glass and a raincoat, and is playing detective. They must be driving poor Dudley mad."

It was true enough that the "Columbos" of St. Augustine read the list and smiled smugly. Only a few items on the official list of evidence came as a surprise.

Evidence included a machete, believed to be the weapon used to butcher Athalia along with several other bush knives that had been confiscated during the investigation; pieces of a man's clothing, a man's watch; and a bag of dried mud the sheriff had removed from the tires of the county car Stanford had driven on the night of the murder. Also, such things as blood stained gravel removed from Stanford's yard, and paper tissues, paper towels and rags, smeared with blood matching that of the victim.

The May 29 motions hearing dragged out for nearly eight hours. Bored reporters and other spectators drifted in and out of the courtroom to smoke or sip soft drinks during periods when attorneys, like broken records, were rehashing the same arguments.

At the defense table, Stanford sat neatly dressed in a light tan business suit and a brown tie. He had lost weight and his eyes were like two empty sockets, circled by dark rings. He was worried. The possibility that he would be sent back to jail was a recurring nightmare. He had heard that prosecutors were under pressure from the public to have his bond revoked and that Boyles was not of a mind to make deals with his defense attorneys. Going back to jail would mean a financial loss because he had just been hired to do carpentry and maintenance work for Dobbs Marina in St. Augustine.

Stanford had managed to evoke a smattering of public sympathy by riding a bicycle the two miles back and forth from his home to the marina where he was working rather than take the family's only car or have his wife drive him back and forth.

The exercise also helped dissipate some of the anger he felt over the disruptions Athalia's death had caused in his life. Because he'd had the misfortune to live next door to a witch, he'd lost his new car, his job, some of the respect he had previously enjoyed in the community and if he failed to convince the jury of his innocence at the upcoming trial, he might lose his life.

His thoughts were interrupted by his attorney, Walter Arnold, handing him a legal sized yellow pad for taking notes. Arnold was a cool cat but sometimes Stanford thought his attorney's face would crack if he ever smiled at him. Maybe smiling was against the rules before a trial. He didn't know. Arnold's assistant, Ed Booth, smiled at him most all the time. They made a strange pair.

Stanford had barely glanced at his wife and his daughter, Patricia, who were sitting nearby with the Rev. Boss. He was afraid his wife was going to suffer a nervous breakdown if the judge put him back in jail. So far, she had held up so well, keeping up appearances by continuing most of her social activities as though nothing had happened.

Stanford was happy to see Boss was wearing his clerical collar. There was no jury to see him but the judge and the press could know that the family minister remained supportive. Boss was as sincerely kind and compassionate as Arnold was tough and unbending. Boss had assured him Arnold was merely preparing him for how it would be if he took the stand and gave the prosecution their field day at the trial. Boss said Arnold's only concern was winning and he was doing what experience had taught him was necessary to achieve that goal.

The priest leaned forward on the bench when the hearing began. Stanford suspected he was praying. The defense won the first round. When Eastmoore denied Boyles' motion to put Stanford back in jail, the Rev. Boss had pulled a white handkerchief from his pocket, wiped his forehead and uttered a sigh of relief. Then, turning to Mrs. Stanford, he whispered: "Man, that was close."

Defense attorney Ed Booth had argued that the state missed the opportunity to get Stanford back behind bars by not asking for a new bond hearing at the time of the indictment or at the hearing afterwards. He said the possibility that a defendant might run away and not appear for trial was the main purpose for denying bond.

"The defendant has given no indication that he intends to flee. He has proven to be a good risk and is currently working every day to support his family," Booth continued.

Eastmoore was not easily convinced but finally, after lengthy contemplation he decided Boyles' reason for revoking bond was insufficient under the circumstances. What bothered Eastmoore was why the state had waited so long before fighting bail. "You passed up your opportunity to keep the defendant in jail," Eastmoore told Boyles. "Now the burden of proof of whether he is entitled to freedom has shifted from the defense to the prosecution."

Next, Eastmoore ruled on the change of venue but only after a lengthy closed door session with Boyles and defense attorneys. It was not clear what had transpired. But, the state lost another round when Eastmoore decided to postpone ruling on moving the trial until "after we have had an opportunity to test the possibility of getting an impartial jury in this county."

The defense gained again when the judge ruled in favor of Arnold's motion that the items seized when sheriff's deputies searched Stanford's house (a few days after the murder) could not be used as evidence against him at the trial. Judge Mathis had issued the warrant authorizing the sheriff to search the Stanford home, but Eastmoore agreed with Arnold that the warrant was invalid because of a technicality. The search warrant was defective in that it failed to direct the sheriff to bring the items seized before the judge. What, in fact, had happened, were the sheriff's department and the prosecutors had used a form for the search warrant which, when it had been reproduced, had inadvertently omitted that essential phrase. Therefore, there was no record, other than a sheriff's department report, of what had actually been taken from the house and grounds during the search.

Garrett said later it was no big deal because the most important and the most damaging evidence he was holding against Stanford had not come from the house search. Items taken during the search included two concrete blocks, spotted with blood and a blood-smeared paper towel. The blood on both supposedly matched Athalia's. Deputies had found the blocks and the towel just outside Stanford's garage.

Garrett said the blocks "didn't mean much because you can't lift fingerprints from concrete."

During the search deputies also had seized the work clothes Stanford was wearing when he returned to his home on the evening of the murder.

The trial had tentatively been scheduled for late May but Eastmoore agreed to Arnold's request for another two-month delay. Arnold said he had been too busy with other cases to search for new witnesses in St. Augustine who could help prove that Stanford was innocent. The delay also had psychological overtones. It allowed more time for the initial shock that followed the brutal murder to wane, making it easier for the defense to select a jury.

Eastmoore had expected to hear from defense attorneys by August 1. He waited another week after that deadline before writing a letter, requesting a progress report on the pre-trial preparations. On August 15 Eastmoore announced he had agreed to another 10-week delay but set November 4 as a new deadline for trial. Reporters shared in Sheriff Garrett's dismay.

"What year?" one of the radio station commentators had asked Eastmoore.

Eastmoore smiled. He knew everyone was weary of waiting but Stanford had waived his rights to a speedy trial. So, Eastmoore was not really surprised when three days before the trial was set to open, Arnold came up with reasons for still another delay, indeed pushing the trial into another year.

At the October 31 hearing, Arnold asked to have nine of the items of evidence collected against Stanford, including the alleged murder weapon and bloodstained clothing, released to the defense for the purpose of sending the items to a private crime laboratory in California for examination. It was an unprecedented motion in the history of pre-trial hearings in St. Johns County.

At first, Eastmoore was skittish about allowing it. "I can foresee all kinds of problems arising from shipping evidence out of this county," he said.

Boyles was outraged by the proposal. Under the law commonly referred to as "discovery," Stanford was entitled to see the cards stacked against him but to Boyles it was unthinkable to allow key pieces of evidence to be shipped across country and to risk loss or alteration of any one of the items. For Eastmoore, it was a question of whether Arnold's proposal was too broad an interpretation of the "discovery" law. But, Arnold had done his homework and had found precedents. Eastmoore granted the motion provided the evidence would be taken to the California laboratory and returned to St. Johns County by a custodian from the St. Johns County Sheriff's Department. Stanford would be required to pay all of the officer's travel expenses. The State was not to pick up the tab for so much as a hamburger.

To allow time for the out-of-state examination, Eastmoore moved the trial date to January 20, 1975, just two days short of a year after the slaying of Athalia Ponsell Lindsey.

Chapter 19

Another Marine Street Murder

The day before Eastmoore set the new January trial date, Shannon Smith lunched with Frances Bemis and Katherine Hawkins.

Frances had made 12:30 reservations at Eddie's Caravan Restaurant, but had invited the guests to her home for what she called "elevensies," a term for pre-noon cocktails she had purloined from the novel, *Please Don't Stop the Carnival*.

Frances made Bloody Mary cocktails for her guests and poured a glass of Port for herself. Then she stood, wearing the expression of one who was about to open the curtain on a cliff-hanger, setting the stage for her announcement that she had invited another guest, a possible witness for the Stanford murder trial, to join the group for lunch.

"After that last county commission meeting Athalia attended, Stanford told this man 'I could slit her throat'. I thought Shannon might convince him he should tell Dick Watson," Frances explained.

The reporter was scheduled to give similar testimony at the trial concerning a telephone call she had received from Stanford about a week before Athalia's murder. The purpose of the call had been to pump her about any thing bad she might know about Athalia's past or her three previous marriages. After Shannon explained she couldn't help him, Stanford had said: "if she does not stop what she is doing to me, I'm going to send her back to where she came from."

"You mean Jacksonville?" Shannon had asked.

"No," Stanford had replied. "I mean back to where she came from."

Shannon was about to tell Frances she was not in a position to solicit witnesses for the state when Frances explained that her mystery man had refused the luncheon invitation because he refused to get involved.

Katherine glared at Frances, angry because her old friend could, at times, be such a tease.

"Did this man also witness the murder?" Shannon asked. Frances did not think so but admitted it was possible. "He lives in the neighborhood."

Shannon pressed for a name but Frances would not say. "I would be betraying a confidence but I will tell you this. I have not given up on this man. I will talk to him again tonight. He lives on my walk route."

"Damn you, Frances, "Katherine scolded, so frustrated that she lit a fresh cigarette, forgetting the one smoking in the ash tray at her elbow. "Why did you say anything at all if you are going to leave us hanging like this?"

Ignoring the remark, Frances turned to Shannon. "We'd better be leaving if you expect to get back to work in time for the school board meeting. Will you drive, my dear?"

That luncheon on October 31 was the last time either Katherine or Shannon would see Frances Bemis alive. They would never learn the name of Frances' witness. Like that of the bushy-haired Oriental who had yelled at Mr. Brunson on the night of Athalia's murder, the man's identity would forever remain a mystery.

Shortly before noon the following Sunday, friends drove Frances and Stanley Osborne to a party at Seminole Beach near Jacksonville. Around 6:30 that evening, Frances and Osborne were dropped off in the driveway of Maria Sanchez Apartment House on Marine Street in St. Augustine. Stanley saw Frances to her door and waited while she fished in her purse for a key before he walked around the house to his private quarters.

It was a little later than Frances normally began her evening walk but she told Stanley she was going to walk anyway as soon as she changed into walking shoes. Osborne did not approve because the sky already was beginning to look inky.

"It would not hurt for you to skip one night of walking," Osborne scolded her.

Frances laughed, "Now, Stanley, no one is going to bother an old lady like me." Osborne sighed. Frances was always saying that. "Well, goodnight, my dear. See you tomorrow." Stanley turned toward the steps, knowing it was useless to argue.

About fifteen minutes later, Frances flicked on the porch light, locked her tacky lavender colored front door, and pinned the door key inside the blouse of her flowered jersey dress. She had removed her jewelry and left it with her purse on the marble top coffee table in the living room, carrying with her only a flashlight and an armful of magazines she planned to drop off at the home of Cathy Hall, who lived five blocks away on Bridge Street.

A new moon provided a faint light in the nearly starless sky as she began walking north on Marine Street, passing Alan Stanford's house and the darkened residence where Athalia had been murdered nearly 10 months earlier. Passing Athalia's place always saddened Frances. It also made her feel a trifle edgy but it did not discourage her from walking. Lights were on in most of the houses along the street that evening but Frances did not stop to ring any doorbells. She went directly to Cathy Hall's rented cottage on Bridge Street where she left the magazines at the door, refusing Cathy's invitation to stay for a visit.

Cathy did not press her to stay. "I guess it is better you get on back home. You really should not be walking alone this late."

Cathy had walked to the edge of the porch where she watched as Frances walked to the intersection of Bridge and North Marine Streets, crossed Marine and turned south on the street.

Cathy wondered why Frances did not walk another block down Bridge toward the bayfront which was better lighted than that northern segment of Marine Street, It really wasn't out of the way to walk the bayfront route because it curved around and intersected with the southern block of Marine Street where Frances lived.

While standing on the porch, Cathy noticed a man standing in the shadows on the southwest corner of Bridge and Marine Streets. He looked familiar but it was really too dark to make out the face. The man was still standing on the corner when Cathy went back inside, pulled the shades and double-checked the locks on windows and doors. Then, she went into the bedroom to begin thumbing through the magazines Frances had left.

Minutes later, an elderly woman who lived in an apartment house on the southeast corner of Bridge and Marine Streets, heard what sounded like a scream coming from outside a downstairs window that overlooked a narrow paved walk, leading from Marine Street to the bayfront.

The window overlooking the walk was slightly open but covered by a blind. Raising the blind an inch, the woman called: "Who's there?" She called again after hearing a faint, childlike voice crying, "No. No. No," followed by shuffling sounds. Too frightened to go outside, the woman closed and locked the window before going to the telephone to call the police department.

St. Augustine Police logged her call at 7:05 p.m. A minute or so later, the dispatcher received a second call from another woman who lived in the same apartment house, relayed the information to an officer in a prowl car who drove immediately to the address given by the two callers. The officer stopped at the corner of Bridge and Marine Streets, looked toward the front of the apartment house without getting out of the car. He then drove halfway down Bridge toward the bayfront where he stopped and surveyed the rear side and the yard of the two story rock structure. Failing to see or hear anything unusual, the officer drove away without stopping to talk with either of the women who had complained.

The dispatcher had not made it clear there was a walkway on the far side of the house, and being new on the force, the young officer was not aware of it. However, if he had parked his car and walked around the house, he would have discovered the path and possibly caught a killer.

Early the next morning, a German Shepherd tugged at his leash and led the woman who was walking the dog along South Marine Street off the sidewalk and across a vacant lot to the bloodied, nearly nude body of a woman, sprawled in the sand of a construction site. The lot was directly across the street from the apartment house where two of the residents had been frightened by noises in the alley the evening before.

As was her custom, Martha Davis, then secretary to Circuit Judge Howell Melton, had risen at six in the morning to take her dog, "Prince" for his morning walk before preparing breakfast and heading up the street to her office at the courthouse.

Martha lived in a large house next door to Cathy's cottage. The body was practically in her backyard. After leading his mistress to the body, "Prince" began to whimper and tried to lie down beside the dead woman, but the hysterical Martha literally drug the 115-pound animal across the vacant lot and around the corner to her house where she bolted the door and called the police.

At 7:15 that same morning, Jean Troemel turned on the kitchen radio to catch Ivan Perry's Early Bird news report on Station WFOY. Perry's main report concerned the discovery of a bludgeoned body of an elderly woman on Marine Street. Immediately, Jean thought of Frances Bemis and ran to the telephone to dial her number. Failing to get an answer, she called Stanley Osborne.

"She doesn't answer her telephone. I have a feeling something is wrong."

Fear stabbed at the pit of Stanley's stomach as he threw a robe over his pajamas and walked around the house where he saw the porch light still burning. Before returning to his apartment, Stanley rang the door bell at least a dozen times. While waiting at the door, the telephone inside began ringing. He counted 20 rings before the bell stopped.

Back in his apartment, Stanley reached for the telephone with trembling hands to tell Jean he did not believe Frances had been home all night.

"She always turns off the porch light when she gets back from her walk. She worries about the electric bill," Osborne explained.

"Just sit tight and try not to worry. I'll get back with you after I check on something," Jean told Stanley.

Jean was standing talking to City Police Officer James Hewitt when Shannon Smith reached the murder scene that morning. Hewitt had borrowed a sheet from one of the neighbors and covered the body of the dead woman. He was doing his best to secure the scene and keep people off the lot until officers, who had been called from the Florida Department of Law Enforcement's Jacksonville office and Chief of Police Virgil Stuart, could get here.

Hewitt had blocked off that section of North Marine Street to vehicular traffic but pedestrians who had heard there had been another violent murder on Marine Street were dropping out of nowhere. To add to Hewitt's problems, a trailer train, coming down Bridge Street, had broken down just as it reached the corner where police cars were blocking the entrance to Marine Street. Tourists had begun bailing out and were swarming on the street like bees on blossoms in an orange grove.

Shannon parked her car behind the disabled train and walked quickly toward the lot where Jean and Hewitt were talking. Reaching them, she whipped out a note-book.

She noted that the shrouded body lay amid tools and piles of building materials including stacks of concrete blocks, apparently awaiting the beginning of construction of a house on the lot. Hewitt said he had found a portion of a concrete block, streaked with blood stains, near the body.

"Who is the dead woman?" Shannon asked Hewitt, repeating a question Jean had asked earlier.

Hewitt said the woman appeared to be elderly but her face was smashed beyond recognition. She was naked except for a piece of flowered jersey, garroted around her neck, a torn bra and a strand of white pearls. She also was wearing one of her shoes--an ecru colored oxford. The mate to the shoe was lying in the walkway across the street, along with a torn flowered jersey skirt and a flashlight. The skirt matched the garment, knotted around the woman's neck. The skirt was a perfect match for one Shannon had seen Frances Bemis wear on at least half a dozen occasions. Later, after Chief Stuart arrived, he pulled away the sheet for Shannon to view the body.

"Is it Mrs. Bemis?" he asked.

The woman was lying partially on her side and her face was badly disfigured. One eye had been gouged. Stuart turned the face slightly and the other almond-shaped eye, familiar to Shannon, was open and staring a lifeless stare.

Poor Frances Bemis, her body was blood streaked and covered with bruises. Some of the skin on her left thigh appeared to have been singed. Nearby was a pile of ashes with remnants of charred cloth.

In his autopsy report, Dr. Peter Lipkovic, the district medical examiner, said the victim died of severe head injuries and that most of the bones of her body had been crushed. An object with a jagged edge, possibly a piece of concrete, had left an imprint on the pelvic areas. Frances Bemis had been pounded to death in the same senseless manner Athalia had been hacked to death just 10 months earlier on the very same street. It was several days after Shannon identified the remains of her friend that police got official identification through dental records that the body was that of Frances Bemis.

The day Frances' body was found, Shannon went with Chief Stuart, three police officers, a Jacksonville television reporter and Stanley Osborne to the Bemis apartment. While there, Shannon showed Stuart where Frances kept a spare key under a paint can in her garage. Frances, just a week earlier, had shown Shannon the hiding place, saying "you should know this in case of an emergency." The key matched one Officer Hewitt had found on a safety pin, half buried in the sand near the body.

Osborne identified the torn flowered garments found at the murder scene as the remains of a two-pieced dress Frances had worn to the Seminole Beach party on Sunday. Osborne said the flashlight looked like one Frances carried and the beads also resembled the ones she wore to the party on Sunday. Osborne also recalled Frances had worn a black neck scarf but the scarf had not been found at the scene. So far, it had not turned up inside the house.

"The scarf is not important unless the killer had a fetish for scarves and took it or possibly the scarf was burned near the body," Stuart speculated.

Osborne, pale as a sheet, had removed his glasses and was rubbing them vigorously with a freshly laundered handkerchief. Surfacing tears were misting the lenses of the glasses.

Stuart was not aware of Osborne's delicate heart condition but he suggested that Osborne go home and rest. Osborne looked relieved.

"Before you go," Stuart said, "Can you tell us a little something about the lady?"

Osborne explained about the close friendship between his wife and Frances. "But, she (Frances) had many other friends. She was very social-minded, liked to entertain and be entertained. She had friends of all ages, sexes and colors. My God, how she loved children . . . and animals."

"What about enemies?" Osborne looked so troubled by the question, Stuart wished he had not asked.

"I cannot think of anyone although I am sure she

made a few when she marched with Martin Luther King back in the 60's. She complained quite a bit about the way the carriage horses were treated in St. Augustine but she was not the only one," was his thoughtful response.

"Was she abrasive?" Stuart pressed.

"I would not say that but she was opinionated."

"Would you call her a Nosy Parker?" the chief pressed.

Osborne frowned. Clearly, he did not approve of the term.

"She was curious--no--interested is the word," he said firmly.

After Osborne left, Stuart personally went through the contents of the drawers of an antique library table. There he found a copy of a recently revised will and a list of people to whom she had left personal gifts. She had no close relatives and had left the apartment house and the bulk of her estate to Bethune-Cookman, a Negro college at Daytona Beach. Osborne also found a folder with paid and unpaid bills and a long list of names, addresses, phone numbers and dates of birthdays and anniversaries. Then, he found the folder that contained notes she had typed about a manuscript someone was in the process of writing. At the top of the page she had typed: "Murder on Marine Street."

In the body of the notes she had written: "Describe all the horrendous details as I saw them--the body, the blood, neighbors emerging to watch--yet, ever so quiet--the police--the arrival of the husband."

The three pages of notes named and commented on almost everyone connected in any way at all with

Athalia Ponsell Lindsley's murder. The comments about Chief Stuart were among the least flattering.

"Please don't be so kind to Virgil Stuart--a known racist--who could have stopped the 1964 racial horror here, but chose to let the red-necks run the situation; chose to arrest Mrs. Peabody and chose to ignore the few whites who tried valiantly to control dissent . . . a situation out of hand because of Virgil refusing to exercise his authority," the chief read without a flicker of emotion.

Near the end, she wrote: "Inject the opinion of a man I know, a good friend of Stanford's, who said he (Stanford) could very well have done it . . . He told me after the last St. Johns County meeting, 'I hate her guts . . . I could cut her throat.'"

Stuart scanned the notes without comment and then dropped them into a big yellow envelope marked evidence.

"Looks like the lady was writing a book," he said to Shannon as she prepared to leave.

Shannon did not tell him she had a copy of the same notes at home. Frances had made the notes after reading a rough draft of a book Shannon was writing.

Chapter 20

Two More Murders

The afternoon of the day Frances was found bludgeoned to death, children playing around and inside a vacant house in a black residential section of King Street found the nude, battered bodies of a middle-aged black couple.

The man and woman were still breathing when the police arrived but the woman died at St. Augustine General Hospital about an hour later without ever regaining consciousness. The man was life-flighted to University Hospital in Jacksonville where he remained in a coma for weeks before he finally died.

Both of the victims had been struck in the face and head with a heavy, sharp-edged instrument. The pair, eventually identified as Charity Merrell and Jack Turner, were found lying on the floor in a room littered with clothing.

Police established that the woman had been employed off and on as a domestic, a fact that gave birth to an erroneous rumor that Charity was Frances Bemis' maid and that Turner had worked as her yard man. Those rumors are still alive though police have never confirmed them. It was possible Charity had worked for Frances at some period but she was not her maid at the time she and Frances were bashed to death. Katherine Hawkins, who had known Frances for years, did not recall Charity ever working for her. The only maid Katherine knew about was Lily Bloom, who had been Frances' cleaning woman for about a decade at the time of Frances' death.

Oddly, the fact that Charity was a member of the grand jury that indicted Alan Stanford in the murder of Athalia Lindsley did not immediately surface and was never a topic for the grapevine. In fact, it was not until months after the Stanford trial that the information was printed by the *Jacksonville City Scope* in a story, alleging a connection between the Lindsley, Bemis and black couple's murders. No source for the information was given but Athalia's sister, Geraldine, admitted to Shannon Smith that she had furnished the pulp magazine with material for the story.

Police Chief Stuart repeatedly stated he did not believe there was a connection between the murder of Athalia and Frances.

Five days after the Bemis murder, Chief Virgil Stuart left for his annual midwinter vacation. Before leaving, he announced that a friend of the victim's who wished to remain anonymous had offered a $500 reward for anyone with information that might help to identify her killer.

It was Stuart's personal opinion that whoever killed Frances was physically strong and possibly mentally deranged. The police chief put out a news release, asking residents to supply names of anyone they might have observed in the downtown neighborhood who matched that description. As a result, investigators holding the fort in Stuart's absence, received an avalanche of letters, typed, printed, handwritten, signed and unsigned. Some letters had drawings of faces instead of names of possible suspects. A number of the named suspects already were known to police as so-called "peeping toms" and street bums who hung around downtown neighborhoods, making nuisances of themselves.

Many suspects were questioned and former Sheriff and Police Officer Francis O'Loughlin to this day believes one of the mentally disturbed street bums questioned was guilty and that someone paid him to kill Mrs. Bemis. It was true money was found on the normally indigent man after Mrs. Bemis' murder, but investigators could never pull together enough evidence to make an arrest.

While the city police continued receiving letters about suspects, Sheriff Dudley Garrett, who was attending FBI school in Virginia at the time Frances was murdered, returned to town and quietly entered the investigation without taking over as he had after Athalia Lindsley was killed. He declined to answer questions posed by members of the news media, insisting that the Bemis murder was "the city's case." The truth was, as he later admitted to Shannon Smith, he had taken the initiative to look into the case because of phone calls he had received from people who believed Athalia and Frances were killed by the same person. Although Chief Stuart insisted there was no connection between the two cases, there were lots of people who did not believe him, including Jim Lindsley.

Around that same time, for reasons that were never clearly explained to the public, Richard Watson returned to the state attorney's office. It was generally believed he returned as a favor to Sheriff Garrett and others who wanted him to assist with the prosecution of Alan Stanford.

Shortly after his return, Watson telephoned Shannon Smith, to say he and State Attorney Stephen Boyles would like to talk to her about the Bemis murder.

Shannon dropped what she was doing, locked her office and walked the two blocks to the St. Johns County Courthouse where Watson and Boyles were waiting in Boyles' second floor office.

Watson came right to the point.

"Was Frances Bemis writing a book? What do you know about it?"

"She was not writing a book," Shannon replied.

"What about the outline Chief Stuart found in her desk? You know about that."

Shannon nodded, smiling. She had always liked Watson and she was happy he was back on the case. She also strongly suspected he had already guessed the answer to his question.

"Yes, I know about it. I have the original of that outline. I am the one writing a book. Frances was just helping by suggesting some changes and additions to what I have written," was her response.

Watson grinned. "I thought as much. We wanted to hear it from you. Thanks for your help."

That was that. The prosecutors never again questioned the reporter about the notes. Oddly, however, for months afterwards, uninformed sources spread the rumor that Frances was writing a book about Athalia's murder and that the book figured in her death.

A few days after Shannon spoke with Watson and Boyles, Alan Stanford attended a vestry meeting at Trinity Parish and early on asked to make an announcement.

He said he wanted everyone to know that the sheriff's office had questioned him about the death of Mrs. Bemis.

"The only thing that surprised me is why they waited so long," he said. "I assure you I am innocent. I did not kill Mrs. Bemis or Mrs. Lindsley. I had no reason to kill either of them."

Stanford said he could prove he was not anywhere "around" at the time either of the women were murdered.

Stanford told investigators he was having supper at the home of Barry Myers, a fellow vestry member, the night Frances was killed. He said Myers and his wife had invited Stanford's daughter Annette, to spend the afternoon with their four-year-old daughter. When the Stanford's went by around 5:30 that afternoon to pick up Annette, the Myers invited them to stay and eat. As well as anyone involved could recall, the Stanford's had stayed at the Myers house until after 7:30 p.m. The estimated time of Frances' death was between 7 and 7:30.

Garrett had confirmed Stanford's story that he and his wife and Annette had stopped off at the home of another vestry member before going home the evening of Frances' murder.

"We didn't find anything at the murder scene to link the deaths of Mrs. Lindsley and Mrs. Bemis but we had to question Stanford because of public pressure," Garrett told Shannon Smith.

"People naturally are trying to link the two killings because both women were victims of over-kill but that proves nothing," Garrett said.

He said he had tried to learn the identity of the man Frances supposedly had been pressuring to testify against Stanford but if the man existed, he could not find him.

The sheriff was aware that Frances had not been a Stanford fan and had made no effort to conceal her opinion that he was guilty of killing Athalia. She had even gone so far as to tell several of her friends, including a neighbor, Sally Buckeley, that she knew "for sure" who killed Athalia. But, as Garrett pointed out, Frances was just one of the dozens of individuals who had made no secret of their feelings concerning his guilt or innocence. Half the town had convicted him before he ever was arrested, Garrett said.

As for Sally, she said she had believed "Frances was just bragging about knowing the killer's identity. She liked to pretend she had inside information on everything. Certainly none of her friends believed she had actually witnessed the attack."

Mabel Long, a woman who lived near Marineland, told a different story to Shannon Smith months after Frances was killed. Mabel said Frances had called her in hysterics a few minutes after six the night of Athalia's murder, begging her to come spend the night.

"She told me she had just witnessed a murder. She had started on her nightly walk and when she got to the Lindsley house, she saw a man in the yard striking Athalia again and again with a sword or some such thing. She had turned around, gone back home and called me."

Mabel's husband, Sid, had driven her to St. Augustine.

"I stayed with Frances three nights. She was willing for me to go home on Saturday morning because an old friend from New York was coming to visit her," Mabel said.

Mabel had first told her story to a city police investigator when she called him concerning another matter possibly relative to Frances' death.

The night before she was killed, Frances had called Mabel "pretty upset."

Mabel recalled, "she had just come from the Bayfront . . . she always walked to that area in the evening . . . and while she was walking a man had come ashore from a boat and demanded money. Of course, she never carried money and had none to give him. But, the man had been angry, made some threats. Frances claimed she had never seen the boater before. She would never come right out and name the man she saw hitting Mrs. Lindsley, but she would always insist, she knew who it was and that it was not Jim Lindsley."

Mabel didn't know why Frances had told so many people she had taken her walk as usual the night Athalia was killed or why she had been so brazen about voicing her opinion as to the identity of the killer.

Nor, did it make sense that Frances would have walked alone the night after the boater had frightened her with demands for money. Had the boater returned and killed her? Was he in some way connected with Athalia's killer?

Mabel told her story to an investigating officer while Garrett was still away at FBI school. For some reason the information never reached the sheriff's office and Mabel was never questioned further. However, when Mabel was called for jury duty at the Stanford trial the following January, she asked to be excused, saying she could not serve "because I was a close friend of Frances Bemis who also was murdered."

Not only did Garrett miss an opportunity to question Mabel, he also missed talking to Cathy Hall, the woman who had seen a man on the corner of Bridge and Marine Streets after Frances left her house on the evening she was bludgeoned in the vacant lot. At the time, Cathy thought the man looked familiar but it was only after she learned of Frances' murder that she considered the possibility the man she had seen was Stanford.

The possibility both confused and terrified Cathy, who had met Stanford at Trinity Parish and had made a small contribution to his defense fund, for which she had caught hell from Frances. Cathy refused to go forward to make a statement to the police because she believed the man standing on the corner the night of the Bemis murder--whoever he might be--had also seen Cathy. If so, and he was the one who killed Frances, then Cathy was in possible danger.

Cathy confided her suspicions only to a relative who lived in Jacksonville. Exactly three weeks after

Frances was killed, Cathy left town without a word to any of her friends about where she was going.

Cathy wrote Shannon Smith once from California where she stayed for more than a year with a sister but there was no return address on the envelope. In her letter, Cathy said she was not coming back to live in St. Augustine until after Stanford was tried for the murder of Athalia Lindsley. As far as anyone knows, Cathy never spent another night in the house on Bridge Street. Sometime in late 1975, she had her furniture moved to the Mandarin home of a Jacksonville relative.

By Christmas of 1974, the probe into the bludgeoning deaths of Mrs. Bemis and the black couple had lost its steam. Three more names were added to the list of unsolved murders in St. Johns County.

Machete, watch, clothing found by Dewey Lee

Location of Homes:
1. McCormick
2. Athalia Lindsley
3. Stanford

Frances Bemis Murdered

INTRACOASTAL

Chapter 21

Selecting A Jury

At 8:45 on the morning of January 20, 1975, there was breathing room only in the hallways leading to the third floor circuit courtroom of the St. Johns County Courthouse.

For at least 30 minutes, elevators, carrying people wedged together like chocolates in a sampler box, had been yo-yoing back and forth between the lobby and the third floor.

Jury selection in the long-awaited trial of Alan Stanford was scheduled to begin at 9:00 a.m.

With nearly 100 of the 250-member venire being called the first day, prospective jurors alone would have constituted a heavier than usual demand for elevator service to the third floor that morning. But, space in the elevator cars also had to be shared with an unusual number of reporters, cameramen and spectators who would be following the courtroom drama like a soap opera.

Spectators probably would have outnumbered members of the venire had Judge Eastmoore not taken steps to prevent day-to-day battling over the courtroom's limited seating capacity. Aware of the widespread interest in the trial and the number of people it would likely attract, Judge Eastmoore, during pre-trial planning, had called a press conference to announce the ground rules for all spectators, including reporters.

No spectator was to be admitted to the courtroom without a pass, signed by Sheriff Garrett. All passes were to be issued three days in advance of the opening of the trial. Contrary to custom in St. Johns County, there would be no coming or going while court was in session. And, there would be no exceptions including reporters with deadlines. All spectators would remain seated until Eastmoore called a recess.

Although Eastmoore had barred television cameras in the courtroom, several news crews, hoisting video equipment, stubbornly clustered like buzzards outside the cubbyhole of a witness room that adjoined the third floor circuit courtroom. The crews moved their positions only to make room for two bailiffs in steam-pressed green uniforms who inched their way through the corridor to unlock the door to the witness room and the main entrance for spectators to the courtroom. Then, as the mob thinned and people with passes began filing into court, the camera crews spread to begin positioning their cameras to focus in on the arrival of the defendant and his entourage of attorneys.

In contrast to the dark-suited attorneys, Stanford wore a light green suit, a near lettuce shade, one of several light-colored suits he wore throughout the trial. His mouth widened into a celebrity-sized smile as he moved into a blinding television spotlight that followed him like a shadow as he trailed his attorney into and through the witness room. Inside the courtroom, which was off-limits to the eyes of television cameras, he took a seat at a long table to the right of the judge's bench. The table directly faced the jury box where the 12 people selected to decide his fate would sit. Twelve at a time, prospective jurors would sit in the box during the lengthy and tiresome process of selecting the panel and two alternates.

It was important for Stanford to watch the expressions on the faces of his prospective judges as attorneys quizzed them about their background, their prejudices, their relationships to anyone involved in the trial, their feelings about capital punishment and any opinions they might have formed regarding the guilt or innocence of the defendant.

The same questions were repeated like a broken record as the lawyers attempted to purge the venire and find a panel acceptable to both prosecutors and defense lawyers. Seating the panel took exactly two and one half days, a considerably shorter period than prosecutors, who had wanted the trial moved to another county, would have believed possible.

Several weeks ahead of the trial, attorneys for the state began preparing a list of names of St. Johns County residents who would not be acceptable to the prosecution as jurors in Stanford's trial, beginning with names of people who had contributed to Stanford's defense fund.

The list was vital to the purge because there was no guarantee that everyone questioned would admit right off to having friendly ties with the defendant. Aside from the problem of trying to identify and weed out members of the venire who wanted Stanford acquitted for personal reasons, prosecutors believed they were further handicapped in the chore of finding 12 people without preset notions about Stanford's guilt or innocence because of the sensational and widespread coverage the media had given the murder. Ideally, attorneys also hoped to spot and eliminate people who were overly anxious to be accepted as jurists, solely out of curiosity or fascination for the bizarre. From the state's point of view, at least, the major purpose of the trial was to inform, not entertain.

So, as the hands of the courtroom clock moved toward 12:30 in the afternoon of January 22, 1975, short just one day of being a full year after the brutal murder of Athalia Ponsell Lindsley, the process of selecting a jury to decide the fate of her alleged killer was completed.

The state had earlier filed a motion to move the trial to another county because of the mega amounts of publicity the case had received, but Eastmoore had ruled to give attorneys three days to pick a panel with the deadline falling at 12:30 on Wednesday, January 22, before he would grant the state's motion. As he later pointed out, "we came within 38 minutes of moving the trial to Volusia County."

The panel--seven men and five women, were seated shortly before Eastmoore recessed the court for lunch. There were three blacks on the jury and two of the jurors walked with canes. Another man and woman were later chosen as alternates who would sit outside the jury box, listening to the trial, preparing themselves to become a member of the historic panel in the event one of the original jurors became ill.

Chapter 22

Long Delayed
Trial Begins

The original list of names state and defense attorneys proposed to call as witnesses at the trial totaled 90.

It was rather an outrageous total compared to the average number of witnesses (20 at most) who were normally heard at murder trials in St. Johns County, and a bit extravagant even for a trial in which the reputations of major public figures were at stake.

The public could only guess at the quantity of testimony necessary when Eastmoore forced a boiling down of the witness pot to nearly half of the original size by limiting trial testimony to 10 days. Eastmoore wanted the trial to be concluded within a week but was willing to stretch the time if there proved to be a reason.

The judge made the decision partly out of consideration for the sequestered jury members. He did not want them locked up a day longer than was necessary but he also hoped to eliminate repetitious testimony or some other ploy on the part of attorneys to try to prejudice the jury.

State Attorney Stephen Boyles was brief and to the point in his opening statement. Boyles said his remarks were intended only as "an eye opener" as to the brutal nature of the crime. He said the state intended to prove former County Manager Alan Stanford had used a machete, borrowed from the county road department, to hack to death his neighbor, Athalia Lindsley, as a result of continued harassment by the victim.

Boyles said Athalia had criticized "the defendant at numerous county commission meetings . . . she actually hell-hacked him and . . . let it be known that she was after his job." In other words, Boyles implied, she had invited Alan Stanford's revenge.

Stanford's attorneys, apparently interested in saving precious time for their witnesses, passed up the opportunity to make a pre-trial statement to the jury.

If one wanted to give an oversimplified summary of the trial, it would be accurate to say that the state used most of its witnesses to try to prove Stanford had a motive to kill Mrs. Lindsley and to break down Stanford's alibi at the time Athalia was attacked. The defense countered by using witnesses to plant seeds of reasonable doubt about Stanford's guilt in the minds of the jury and to try and shift the guilt to two of the state's own witnesses.

Athalia's fourth husband, former Mayor James Lindsley, was one of the witnesses the defense attempted to use as a scapegoat. The other witness was Dewey Lee, the county road department employee who turned in the machete and bloody clothes that led to Stanford's arrest.

The state called Lindsley to the stand on Monday, January 27. When he stepped into the witness box, he was wearing a grey business suit, white shirt and black tie. Intentionally or not, the suit matched the ashen color of his face and set the stage for Assistant State Attorney Richard Watson's line of questioning, aimed at suggesting to the jury that James Lindsley was in poor health, not physically capable of striking the blows that killed his wife.

Watson quickly managed to establish that the 65-year-old Realtor was a three-time cancer victim and had undergone several abdominal operations before his marriage to Athalia. From his place at the defense table, Stanford kept his eyes glued on Lindsley during the more than two hours the former mayor sat in the witness box. If Stanford expected Lindsley to become unstrung at some point by Stanford's attorneys repeated attempts to demonstrate to the jury that there had been animosity between Lindsley and his slain wife, he was disappointed.

Under cross examination, but out of the ear shot of jurors whom Eastmoore temporarily ordered from the courtroom at one point, Walter Arnold had waded into Lindsley by asking if he owned a machete. Then, Arnold had whipped out a black-handled weapon from a purple cover and tried to get Lindsley to say it was the same machete he had carried in the back of his car prior to the murder.

"Have you ever seen it before?" Arnold asked. Lindsley leaned forward to peer through black-rimmed reading glasses at the weapon Arnold was holding.

"I can't positively identify it as mine. All weapons look alike to me," he replied. Lindsley was again asked to try and identify the machete after Eastmoore called the jury back into the courtroom. The second time Lindsley was questioned, the weapon was not visible to people in the courtroom. Eastmoore had ordered it placed in a large paper bag and Lindsley was called from the stand to look into the bag.

"Is that the machete you turned over to the sheriff's department?" Stanford's attorney asked. Again, Lindsley said he could not be sure. "It looks similar to one I owned," he said finally before returning to the stand where he began answering a new series of questions posed by Walter Arnold.

Arnold asked, "Did she (Athalia) call you a liar and a thief on the day of her death?"

Watson objected to the question before Lindsley could answer and Eastmoore ordered it struck from the record but the question could not be erased from jurors' minds.

Arnold was successful in getting Lindsley to admit he had once removed a $50 check from an envelope his wife had asked him to mail for her. The envelope and the check were addressed to a radio evangelist in Minnesota. Lindsley said the envelope Athalia had asked him to mail was not sealed and he had removed the check because helping a "radio preacher seemed a whimsical thing to do."

Arnold shook his head disapprovingly. "It was her business wasn't it?"

"I suppose so," Lindsley replied.

Later in his testimony, the former mayor denied having argued with his wife the afternoon before she was killed. Arnold then asked Lindsley how he was dressed that afternoon when he and the victim returned from Jacksonville. Lindsley did not answer immediately. He seemed to be trying to remember.

Finally he described his attire as a blue shirt and tie and a pair of maroon trousers. But, when Arnold suggested the shirt was white, Lindsley admitted it "could have been." There were lots of white shirts in his wardrobe.

Arnold also asked what Mrs. Lindsley was wearing on the day of her murder. After some waffling, he finally got around to the main question: "Did she wear underpants?"

Without hesitating, Lindsley replied: "Not if she could help it."

It was never brought out in pre-trial news stories that Athalia was not wearing underpants when her body was discovered. Police had withheld the information, mostly because they did not consider it pertinent since she had not been raped. They had learned from Lindsley that during her years as a model, Athalia had stopped wearing undergarments that might cause a bulge or line under her clothes. Arnold dropped the subject before Jim could explain at the trial.

Lindsley remained outwardly calm when Arnold suddenly began interrogating him about his first marriage and the death of his first wife. It was true, Lindsley admitted, that he had divorced and then remarried his first wife, Lillian, and that he had been at the wheel of the car when she was fatally injured in an automobile accident on New Year's Day in 1971.

Lindsley testified he had known Athalia about five months prior to their five-month marriage. He insisted the brief marriage had been a good one although he and Athalia had maintained separate residences. Under questioning by Arnold, he admitted the couple had one small disagreement over who was entitled to file homestead exemption. In Florida, property owners are entitled to the homestead reduction in taxation on property in which they live. Lindsley said they settled the argument when he agreed Athalia could file for the exemption.

Lindsley described their first Christmas together as "wonderful." He recalled giving his wife a $100 dress, a diamond ring that had belonged to his mother and a pair of jade earrings. He said he also had made a new will, naming Athalia to share his estate equally with his only living son.

If this were true, Arnold interjected, turning to face the jury, why had Mrs. Lindsley changed the locks to the front and back door at her home on Marine Street without giving her husband a set of new keys and why had she disinherited Lindsley in her will?

Lindsley said Athalia had changed locks because she was terrified of burglary and that she had given him keys for the new locks but he had misplaced them. At least, Lindsley, said, he had not been able to find them after her murder.

Arnold asked about the keys because Alan Stanford had told his lawyer about seeing Lindsley and Sheriff's Lt. Eddie Lightsey break into the back door of Athalia's home a few days after she was murdered.

Stanford had been standing at the kitchen window watching when Lightsey kicked in the door and entered the house with Lindsley.

Lindsley then admitted he had forced his way into the house after Athalia's sister, Geraldine, had come and moved out furniture without consulting him. He said he wanted to make an inventory of what was left.

Finally, Arnold forced Lindsley to admit that two weeks after Athalia's death, he had filed a petition, asking to have her will set aside because she had left all of her possessions to her sister, Geraldine Horton, of Honolulu. However, Lindsley said with a shrug, he and Mrs. Horton reached an agreement to split the estate 50-50.

Eastmoore ordered the jury from the room before allowing Arnold to continue questioning Lindsley about Athalia's estate. In the absence of the panel, Arnold accused Lindsley of knowing his wife was not going to include him in her new will because he had been with her when she was discussing it with her attorney. But, Lindsley said he had not known for sure because he was excluded from the legal discussions. Arnold inferred that he could prove Lindsley knew he was about to be disinherited by calling another witness, but as it turned out, he did not and Eastmoore banned discussion about the will before the jury.

Chapter 23

Eyewitness
Gives Testimony

Prosecutors had opened the trial by trying to establish, through witnesses, that Athalia Ponsell Lindsley not only had been murdered by Alan Stanford, she had been the victim of a vicious overkill. One of the two medical technicians who reached the scene ahead of the police, testified that ambulance attendants had been so shocked and sickened by the excessive amount of blood that had spouted and flowed from the victim's wounds, one of the attendants had grabbed the garden hose and tried to wash some of the splatters off the porch and steps.

Dr. Arthur Schwartz, medical examiner for Florida's fifth judicial district, explained the reason for the victim's excessive blood loss. Schwartz told the jury the assailant struck and cut Mrs. Lindsley at least nine times with a heavy thick-bladed knife, one of the blows nearly decapitating her. It was the examiner's opinion that the weapon used was a bush knife, more commonly known in North America as a machete.

The doctor testified that deep slashes, extending from the back of Mrs. Lindsley's head into the skull and the base of her neck had severed one of four main arteries going to the brain, and that blows to the right arm had nearly amputated Athalia's forearm and wrist. Schwartz did not believe that a smaller knife would have penetrated the bone in such a manner. He said the use of a meat cleaver or an axe would have left different types of slashes and bruise marks on the body.

The doctor pictured the victim as having been standing on the porch or the top step when the attack began and perhaps lifting her right arm to protect her face when the killer began swinging the knife. He speculated that Athalia had fallen as the blows continued and was on the ground when "the enormous cuts in the skull and neck were delivered." As Schwartz spoke, Stanford sat immobile as a statue, his face grey as granite, his expressionless eyes glued on the witness.

Schwartz was introduced as an expert witness and Defense Attorney Arnold agreed with prosecutors on that one point. Arnold was obviously disappointed that the examiner had not been so positive the murder weapon used by Athalia's killer was a machete. After Schwartz was excused, prosecutors introduced a series of black and white photographs, taken of the victim after she was slashed to death. Arnold said those pictures were too inflammatory to be shown to the jury, but Judge Eastmoore disagreed, partly because the bloody scenes were not in color.

As the photographs were passed from juror to juror, spectators watched with intense curiosity for some kind of reaction. Members of the panel would have made excellent poker players. Not a flicker of shock, not even the crinkle of a frown, crossed any of the faces. What any one of those jurors was thinking was anyone's guess.

That afternoon saw reporters scrambling out of the courtroom in their first real display of excitement following the testimony of Lucille Smith, the grandmother of the young man who had witnessed a part of the attack on Athalia. Eastmoore had called a recess after Lucille left the stand, red-eyed from crying. Testifying had been a traumatic experience. Lucille was terrified that things she was forced to say about Stanford would infuriate him.

Assistant State Attorney Watson had quickly established that Mrs. Smith was the grandmother of Locke McCormick, who had called the police after witnessing the attack on Athalia Lindsley; that she lived directly across the street from the murdered woman; and that she had witnessed some of the bickering between Athalia and her neighbors.

At Watson's request, Mrs. Smith traced her movements as well as she could remember on the evening of the slaying. She said she had gone grocery shopping that afternoon and left the supermarket about 20 minutes past five to drive home. Turning into her driveway, she had seen Mrs. Lindsley in her yard "between the front steps and the gate." She recalled seeing the crippled bluejay hopping around in the yard.

Mrs. Smith had not looked at her watch but she "guessed" it had been around 5:30 when she parked the car and began unloading groceries. She had put the food away and then walked across the street to her daughter's home. She recalled going into the kitchen to keep her daughter, Rosemary, company while she finished preparing dinner. She guessed it was around six o'clock when she heard the strange noises coming through the open window from next door. "I think it was three chopping sounds," she said.

When Watson asked her to explain the sounds, Mrs. Smith asked if she could use her hands to demonstrate and then proceeded to begin striking her palms together several times in rapid succession. Then, Mrs. Smith said she also had heard moaning not as loud as the chopping noise. "It wasn't a scream I heard. It was more like a muffled moan," she said.

At that point, her voice began to falter and tears surfaced in her eyes as she explained about following her daughter into the den, looking for her grandson, Locke.

Not finding him, the two women had gone to the front door, opened it and, after going outside, had spotted him standing by the fence near Athalia Lindsley's house. As they stood on the porch, Locke had turned around and bolted back toward the house, Mrs. Smith said.

She testified that she had never seen Locke so upset. "He was terribly excited," Lucille Smith recalled. It was at that dramatic point, with Mrs. Smith in tears, Watson proposed that Judge Eastmoore send the jury from the room on the chance that the judge might not consider what the witness was about to say as admissible as evidence.

Once the jury had left the box, Watson, ever so gently, urged that Mrs. Smith tell Eastmoore what her grandson said when he returned to the house. She hesitated, more tears clouding her eyes. Swallowing several times, she finally spit it out, carefully avoiding looking at Alan Stanford.

In that moment of excitement, Locke had identified Athalia's assailant, saying, "Mr. Stanford is hitting Mrs. Ponsell."

Mrs. Smith said she supposed that Locke had called Athalia "Mrs. Ponsell" out of habit because her marriage to Jim Lindsley had been so recent.

Stanford's attorneys objected immediately to the "hearsay testimony" but Watson said he had researched the law and it was his contention that the statement would be admissible before a jury because it was made in a moment of great and unusual excitement. As it turned out, Eastmoore agreed but not immediately. He wanted to think about it overnight.

When the jury returned to the box, Mrs. Smith remained on the stand for only a few minutes, quietly weeping as she answered a few more questions. Watson wanted to know whether she had seen anyone in the yard while Locke was inside his house calling the police. Apparently, Athalia's killer had disappeared because Mrs. Smith only recalled seeing her daughter, Rosemary, talking to Patti Stanford. She said she had called to Rosemary, insisting that she come back inside.

"What were you afraid of?" Watson asked.

"I was frightened for her . . . I was afraid Rosemary might see something horrible," was her trembling answer.

Lucille left the courtroom, head bowed, assisted by the bailiff. Meantime, Rosemary called two Florida National Guardsmen who escorted Lucille from the courthouse to her Marine Street home. The escorts were friends of Rosemary's husband who was a full-time colonel in the Florida National Guard. Because Lucille was in poor health and obviously shaken after her testimony, Rosemary did not want her mother driving herself even the few blocks from the courthouse to Marine Street.

Mrs. Smith's testimony that Locke had blurted out the name of the person he saw hitting Athalia took reporters by surprise. The news media had been led to believe Locke could not identify the killer. What he had said to his grandmother the evening of the murder was possibly the best kept secret of the investigation. When Mrs. Smith returned to the witness box the following day and, at the instruction of Judge Eastmoore, began repeating, before the jury her testimony of the previous day, she remained dry-eyed and composed. Her manner was as casual as that of someone answering questions about something of as little significance as the weather. Once Watson established for the panel that Locke had blurted out the name of the defendant as the man he saw hitting Athalia, Watson then asked Mrs. Smith why she and Locke had withheld that information from investigators who came to the McCormick home the evening of the murder.

Mrs. Smith said she didn't know unless it was because it had been such a confusing evening with police asking so many questions. She recalled interrupting the questioning just one time to ask a question of her own. Lucille had wanted to know if Mrs. Lindsley had been shot.

After excusing Mrs. Smith, prosecutors called Locke McCormick to the stand, asking him to repeat, under an oath, what he had told his grandmother as he ran from the murder scene to call the police.

Without hesitation, Locke admitted yelling in the presence of his mother and grandmother that "Mr. Stanford was hitting Mrs. Ponsell." Locke said he had not told the police because, after thinking it over, he could not be 100 percent sure the man he had seen was Stanford.

"I only saw the shoulders of a man wearing a white shirt," Locke said.

Watson quickly fired the next question: "What was he doing?"

"He was making downward motions with his arm," Locke said.

Watson nodded and then asked Locke to tell the jury what he had done after that. Locke explained that he had walked a little closer to the fence and watched as the man who had been hitting Athalia began walking slowly away, disappearing around the corner of Athalia's house that was nearest to the Stanford home next door.

Under further questioning, Locke said he had assumed the man in the white shirt was Stanford because Stanford often wore white dress shirts. Like Stanford, the man Locke saw was also slightly balding, he said.

Under cross examination by defense attorneys, Locke told about being submitted to hypnosis a few days after the murder in an effort to identify the man in the white shirt. He said Sheriff Garrett had taken him to the office of a hypnotist in Daytona Beach.

Judge Eastmoore allowed Arnold to play a transcript from a tape made at the session with the hypnotist in which Locke had indicated he could not positively identify the man he saw hitting Athalia Lindsley. The voice of Locke on tape stated that the man he saw appeared to be "bigger" than Stanford. Locke thought the man's shoulders were broader and flatter than those of Stanford and that there was something different about the man's hair.

Under re-direct questioning by Watson, Locke admitted he and his father, Connie McCormick, had gone fishing with Stanford a few months after the murder. Although Locke swore he did not recall the three of them discussing the murder, he did remember Stanford and his father talking about McCormick's hunting trip to Mexico with County Commissioner Fred Green. One of the Yucatan newspapers had carried an Associated Press account of the Lindsley murder. After reading it, McCormick had cut short the hunting trip and flown home.

Locke said nothing to the jury about his mother calling his father the night of the murder, ordering him home. Only a few people including McCormick's hunting companion, Commissioner Green, knew of that phone call.

As Locke McCormick exited the courtroom, Stanford caught his eye and smiled.

Chapter 24

Motive For Murder

On Friday, January 24, Assistant State Attorney
Watson devoted most of the day to introducing witnesses
who could testify about the feud between Athalia Lindsley
and her accused killer, and hopefully pin down a motive
for premeditated murder, a charge the state was attempt-
ing to prove.

Prosecutors introduced two witnesses who had not
previously been mentioned by the news media in the
wide-spread publicity, but only by rumor mongers who
kept the gossip going. The witnesses were from the
Florida State Board of Engineers and Land Surveyors and
they were called to tell the jury that they had visited
Stanford at his office, less than two hours before Athalia
was murdered, to warn him that he must stop signing

198 • Bloody Sunset in St. Augustine

county documents, using the title of county engineer, or the state would have to take disciplinary measures.

A state agent, Elmer Emrich, testified first, recalling that he and Thomas Murphy, Jr. arrived at the county road department at about quarter after four on the afternoon of the murder. They had talked to Stanford and left about an hour later. The time of departure was estimated at ten minutes past five in the afternoon. Emrich testified that Stanford had acknowledged he was wrong in signing documents as county engineer. Emrich said that although Athalia had written to the board of engineers, complaining about Stanford, her name was not mentioned that afternoon. Emrich said there was no doubt in his mind that Stanford knew who had instigated the complaint. Asked to describe how Stanford was dressed that afternoon, Emrich said, "he was wearing a long-sleeved white shirt and dark trousers."

When Murphy testified, he described Stanford's attire as "a long-sleeved white shirt and dark wash and wear pants, patterned with a red stripe." Murphy said he specifically recalled the trousers because they did not match the quality of the shirt.

The state considered Murphy's statement important because the dark trousers that were found in the swamp, prior to Stanford's arrest, were also designed with a narrow red stripe. Prosecutors also used the testimony to illustrate that Stanford had good reason to be angry with Athalia on the evening she was murdered.

Stanford's attorneys made no attempt to discredit the memory of the two witnesses but the lawyers did manage to get Emrich to say Stanford had not appeared hostile when they confronted him.

Emrich said Stanford was "calm and collected. . . a gentleman, absolutely no doubt about it."

Two other witnesses that same afternoon were newspaper reporters who had covered the stormy county commission meetings at which Athalia had registered so many bitter complaints about Stanford and his failure to pass the state examination that would have certified him as a civil engineer.

Jackie Feagin, a *St. Augustine Record* reporter, carrying an armful of notebooks to the stand, testified first. Her voice quivered as she read the dates of Mrs. Lindsley's appearances before the board. One of the dates she cited was Oct. 9, 1973.

Watson asked what had happened on that date. Flipping pages in her notebook, Jackie testified that Athalia had stood up, pointed a finger at Stanford and said: "My life has been threatened. He threatened my life."

Asked how Stanford had reacted, Mrs. Feagin said, "He tried to deny the charge but was stopped from making any further statements by the chairman of the county commission."

During cross examination by defense attorneys, Mrs. Feagin said Stanford "always behaved like a gentleman when Mrs. Lindsley criticized him." Although Jackie Feagin was a witness for the prosecution, ironically years later she stated she did not believe Stanford was capable of the murder.

Shannon Smith was the second reporter to testify. She was not happy about being called for a number of reasons. Prior to the murder, she had been socially friendly with Stanford. They had attended the same church and many of the same gatherings for civic leaders and the press. Shannon had been invited to the wedding and reception of the Stanfords' oldest daughter, Sherrie, the previous summer. However, Stanford had not been friendly with Shannon since she had called him on the evening of Athalia's murder, trying to locate Jim Lindsley. In addition too further damaging her relationship with Stanford, Shannon's appearance as a witness prevented her from covering the trial for the *Florida Times-Union*. Being told she could not cover the trial was one of the biggest disappointments of her newspaper career.

The state established that Shannon was a veteran reporter of over 20 years, who during a stint in Jacksonville, had met Athalia Ponsell and her mother, Margaret Fetter. Watson also established that Shannon was acquainted with Stanford and very much aware of the growing feud between Athalia and Stanford and of the victim's campaign to get him removed as county manager.

Shannon's testimony was printed almost verbatim under the byline of Steve Thomas, a reporter for the *Jacksonville Journal*, in the January 25, 1975 edition of the newspaper.

The story read as follows: "Unable to get any dirt on his political antagonist, Athalia Ponsell Lindsley, Alan Stanford hacked her to death just moments after state agents investigated him at her request, the state sought to prove yesterday."

"The murder on Jan. 23, 1974, came just a week after Stanford told newspaper reporter Shannon Smith that he would send Lindsley back to where she came from if she did not stop hounding him."

"You mean back to Jacksonville?" Shannon asked Stanford in a telephone conversation. "No, I mean back to where she came from," the reporter testified that Stanford had replied.

Mrs. Smith testified that Stanford had called her at home to inquire if she knew of any "dirt" on Mrs. Lindsley . . . anything bad about her. Stanford also wanted to know the names of Athalia's ex-husbands.

"He (Stanford) said he had to get something bad on her. I didn't know anything," Shannon testified.

Asked why she had not called the sheriff to relate the phone conversation at the time it happened, Mrs. Smith said she did not think it was necessary because the sheriff was aware that Athalia had accused Stanford of threatening her life at a public county commission meeting. "And, I did not want to become involved in their feud," Mrs. Smith added.

After Shannon Smith left the stand, the state called Stanford's 19-year-old daughter, Patricia.

State Attorney Boyles explained that he was calling Patricia as a witness of the court, rather than the state, because "I cannot vouch for her credibility."

Boyles said he intended to impeach parts of earlier testimony she had given in a deposition to prosecuting attorneys.

Patricia was a curvaceous brunette, a younger version of her mother, Patti. She entered the courtroom, wearing a brown and white mini-dress that hugged her trim figure and showed off her long legs. After climbing into the witness box, she looked directly at her father and proffered a smile.

Patricia testified that she had gone to play tennis with a friend, Hunter Barnett, on the afternoon of the murder. Patricia's mother had driven the girls to municipal

tennis courts off Highway U. S. 1, North, at about two
o'clock.

Patricia said her mother and her three-year-old
sister, Annette, had gone grocery shopping before returning to the courts to pick up Hunter and Patricia about
quarter of five. Then, the Stanfords had driven Hunter
home and arrived back at their Marine Street house about
15 minutes past five.

"Was anyone at home when you arrived?" Boyles
asked.

"Yes, my father was in the kitchen," she answered.

At this point Boyles began an attempt to discredit
the witness, reminding her that in her deposition, the day
after the murder, she said her father was not home when
she and Mrs. Stanford returned but had arrived 15 minutes
later. Patricia shrugged, saying she had been confused and
sleepy when she was called to the courthouse the morning
after the murder. She insisted that her testimony before
the jury was "the truth."

She said her father had returned to his office about
quarter of six that afternoon after telling her mother to
hold supper until he returned.

When Watson took over questioning for the state,
he asked what Patricia had done after her father left.

"I went to the window and looked out. I heard
Rosemary McCormick calling out hysterically." However,
she said she had not seen anything. Afterwards, she said
her mother asked her to take care of "the baby," her little
sister Annette.

"I grabbed the baby and went upstairs. Then, I
looked out of the window and saw Mrs. Lindsley lying

there (in her yard) and my mother and Rosemary standing near the street."

Then, Patricia said she had grabbed her sister and run back downstairs, taking her to swing in the yard. She had gone back inside after her mother came to tell her that Mrs. Lindsley had been murdered. Under questioning, she admitted her mother had not tried to call her father at his office to relate what had happened.

"Why not?" Watson asked.

Patricia shrugged. "We knew he would be back soon."

Later, she estimated it was almost seven in the evening when her father returned. She also admitted that she had dated Locke McCormick prior to the murder and had gone to his house the evening Athalia was killed.

"Why?" Watson asked.

"I had heard rumors he had seen the murder," Patricia explained.

When Watson asked Patricia to repeat what Locke said, one of Stanford's attorneys jumped to his feet to object.

After much arguing between defense and prosecuting lawyers, Patricia was allowed to testify that she and Locke had discussed the identity of the man Locke had seen hitting Mrs. Lindsley. But, by evoking the "hearsay law," Arnold was able to prevent Patricia from having to tell the jury the name of the man Locke said he had seen bending over Athalia.

When Patricia's tennis partner, Hunter, was called to the stand, her testimony conflicted slightly with what Patricia had told the jury.

According to Hunter Barnett, Mrs. Stanford had taken her home between five-thirty and quarter of six, later than Patricia had estimated. Hunter recalled taking a quick shower and stepping out just as the six o'clock news was coming on television. Her stepfather, Jesse Miller, also testified that his daughter returned from the tennis game about quarter of six that evening, but no earlier. Miller said he was sure of the time because he had just come home from fishing at 4:40 and was cleaning out his car when the Stanford car drove up.

Mrs. Patricia Stanford took the stand the following Thursday as a defense witness. She backed up the time frame given by her daughter in court, placing Stanford at the kitchen sink at five-fifteen when she and her daughter returned after dropping off Hunter Barnett. As was his custom, Mrs. Stanford said her husband changed into work clothes and mixed himself a drink.

The time differences given by witnesses concerning Stanford's movements on the afternoon of the murder was puzzling and testimony that followed only added to the confusion.

City Police Officer Francis O'Loughlin testified that Stanford had told him he got home from work about ten minutes past five, the same time the engineering board representatives said they had left him at his office. O'Loughlin said Stanford told him he had looked out the kitchen window a few minutes after arriving home and seen Mrs. Lindsley working in the yard. Testimony of the victim's husband, Jim, indicated she had not arrived until after five-thirty.

Chapter 25

A Bag Full of Evidence

The state waited until mid-trial--Tuesday, January 28--to show jurors the murder weapon, a razor-edged machete Stanford was accused of using to silence Athalia Ponsell Lindsley forever.

Two days after Garrett announced his offer of a $500 reward for evidence, Dewey Lee, a mechanic for the county road department, had turned in the weapon along with a plastic bag, containing, among other things, pieces of bloodstained clothing. Lee had recovered the machete and the plastic bag from a marsh off Riberia Street, a few blocks west of the murder scene. The area had once been used by the city of St. Augustine for dumping garbage. The contents of the bag included a bloody long-sleeved white shirt, a pair of dark trousers designed with a red stripe, a wrist watch, shoes, belt, tie and an assortment of rags, including a baby diaper, spotted with paint and blood.

The shirt had been traced to Stanford through a laundry mark, and the pants were linked to the defendant by a merchant. Ken Beeson, who later became mayor of St. Augustine, testified he had sold Mrs. Stanford a pair of dark blue pants, with a burgundy pin stripe, identical to those recovered from the marsh, several months prior to the murder of Athalia Lindsley. Through records on file at his jewelry store, Charles Tanner identified the watch found in the marsh as the one Stanford had brought to him for repair in 1971. As for the diapers and rags, prosecutors alleged the smears of paint matched the paint on the recently painted walls of the kitchen in the Stanford home.

The calling to the stand of Dewey Lee, who had collected a $500 reward for recovering the items, opened the door for another attempt by defense attorneys to shift the guilt for the crime to someone other than Stanford.

James Lindsley had been the first target although like Lee, Lindsley was shorter in build and had whiter hair than Stanford's. Locke McCormick had described the killer as just under six feet tall with graying hair. Stanford was about six feet and Lindsley and Lee were just under five feet, nine inches.

Rumor had it that Lee had a drinking problem and that prosecutors were edgy about his court appearance. However, the stocky, gray haired witness appeared to be as sober as Judge Eastmoore himself when he took the stand, wearing a suit, white dress shirt and tie. Lee testified that he had read about the reward offer in the February 16, 1974 issue of the *St. Augustine Record*.

Early the next morning, he had taken his dog and driven to "the old city dump" off Riberia Street. The city no longer disposed of garbage there but Lee was aware that some people illegally used the area as a dump.

Lee told the jury that he had parked his car and walked West off the road, past the dumping area and toward a tidal marsh, fed by the San Sebastain River. Then, he had walked South along the East bank of the river and was about a block from a boat works building when he spotted a package in the marsh, "wrapped in a towel with a piece of belt sticking up." The bundle was so deep in the mud, he had to find old boards to use for walking out to get it, Lee told the jury.

"The area was so soft I don't think a bird could have landed on it. The machete was laying in the mud about 10 feet from the package," Lee said.

Defense Attorney Ed Booth suddenly came to life. In a voice, edged with sarcasm, he asked why Lee should begin his search by going directly to the marsh area.

Lee shrugged, as though dismissing the question. He then stated that it had seemed to him the marsh was a logical spot to dispose of a murder weapon without being seen. Too, he added, it was not far from where "the lady was murdered." Lee was not asked if he also was aware that Stanford was familiar with the area and was storing a boat he owned in a nearby building.

Lee's reasoning seemed to amuse Booth, who raised his voice slightly to be sure the jury heard him when he challenged the response by suggesting it was Lee who threw into the swamp the articles he turned in to the sheriff and that he chose the area believing he would not be observed retrieving them.

"Isn't that true?" Booth pressed.

"No," Lee replied firmly.

Booth then began grilling Lee about his relationship with Stanford and did get him to admit he had been to the Stanford residence on several occasions prior to the murder.

Lee said Stanford had called him several times to his Marine Street home to bring jumper cables on occasions when he could not get the car (furnished him by the county) started. In response to Booth's other questions, Lee said he knew about a road department machete Stanford sometimes carried in the back of the county vehicle. But, he glared at Booth, as though to say: "So what? Lots of people knew about that machete."

As the grilling continued, Booth asked about Lee's World War II experience. He asked if Lee used a machete while he was stationed in New Guinea with the Navy. He also asked if Lee had suffered head injuries at that time. He suggested that as a result of head injuries, Lee could not handle alcohol and sometimes went wild while drinking.

Lee said it was true he had a problem with alcohol but he firmly denied Booth's suggestion that he had been drinking the night Athalia was killed.

During Lee's testimony, the court's exhibit of clothing and other items turned into Sheriff Garrett were spread before Lee for identification. Lee said everything looked the same except for the shoes. "I only recall seeing one shoe. It was so muddy I could not tell for sure, but this shoe does not look like the one I saw. The particular shoe I saw, had a cut on the toe. These don't have a cut."

Lee's testimony about the shoes was interesting in view of the fact that during their review of the evidence, jurors would ask to see the shoes Stanford wore to the trial and would note they were size 10 C, slightly larger than the 9 1/2 D shoes in the exhibit of clothing, supposedly discarded by the killer.

Lee testified that after finding the weapon and the clothing, he immediately called Lt. Eddie Lightsey of the St. Johns County Sheriff's Department to make arrangements "to turn the stuff in."

Lightsey was not called to testify at the trial but had given a deposition, stating that he was not on duty the morning Lee called him at home after making his discovery.

Lightsey said he was asleep when Lee telephoned and questioned why Lee was bothering him.

"He (Lee) said 'come on down here in the woods, back here, end of Riberia. I got something I want to show you in the creek,'" Lightsey recalled.

The marsh creek Lee referred to was west of the city's water pollution control plant.

"He (Lee) said he thought he had found what I was looking for, that's what he said."

Lightsey said he asked Lee what he had found, but he wouldn't tell him on the telephone.

"If you show me a West Augustiner that will tell you something on the phone, I will be surprised."

Lightsey said it was only after he met Lee at the marsh site that he told him he had found a machete, nearly covered by mud. Further out in the marsh, he had spotted a towel-wrapped bundle, which contained clothing.

Before dismissing Lee, Booth asked the witness if he had known Mrs. Lindsley.

"Not personally. From the newspaper pictures, I recognized her as someone I had seen," Lee responded.

Through cross-examination, Booth established that Lee had left work at the county road department about five-thirty the afternoon Athalia was killed, but Lee could not recall for sure whether he had gone downtown after work to pick up shoes at a repair shop or if he had gone directly home to cook dinner for his two daughters.

After Lee stepped down, there was testimony that Stanford had asked a county employee, Freddy Hudnall, to put a machete in his car about two months prior to the murder.

The witness who testified was David Wehking, a draftsman for the county. He said he was present at the time Hudnall sharpened the instrument and put it into the back seat of Stanford's county vehicle.

Wehking also testified that on the day after the murder, Stanford had asked him to find the machete he had borrowed earlier. Wehking said Stanford swore he had put it back in the survey truck where road department machetes were stored. There was no record that he had returned the machete and the supply truck was one machete short.

Booth asked if the truck where the machetes were stored was always locked. Wehking said it was only unlocked when the truck was being serviced at the county garage.

Chapter 26

Defense Goes On Offense

Chief Defense Attorney Walter Arnold made his first statements to the jury early on the morning of January 30. Now that panelists had heard the witnesses in the state's case against his client, he was ready to make his declaration that prosecutors had no conclusive evidence connecting Alan Stanford with the murder of Athalia Lindsey. Arnold padded as noiselessly as a man in his stocking feet from the defense table to the podium, facing the jury box.

Prosecutors are out "to get Alan Stanford," he said in a voice resembling that of a father addressing misguided children. The defendant was a fall guy, singled out by investigators who had looked no further than next door for a suspect. Evidence would prove that Stanford had been targeted from the night of the murder despite the fact "he had absolutely nothing to do with this."

Arnold explained in a voice emoting deep concern that there are witnesses who can prove the state had focused "early and prematurely on a man who still remains free under bond." Arnold paused, letting the jury digest the information that the defendant the state was calling a butcher had not spent one day behind bars since his arraignment in county court a year earlier. Arnold reminded the jury that "lo and behold, three weeks after Mrs. Lindsley was hacked to death . . . and after the sheriff offered a $500 reward, a state witness comes up with a neat little package and a machete."

It was only fair, Arnold continued, to make the jury aware that some of the testimony of state witnesses was based on "half truths," including the testimony of one newspaper reporter who said Stanford had told her in a telephone conversation that he was going to send Athalia Lindsley back to where she came from. Arnold said the reporter had misunderstood because, like most women and reporters, she had a tendency to get things half right. Actually, Arnold explained, what Stanford had said was he "wished" Athalia would go back where she came from.

According to Arnold, Stanford had called Shannon Smith to ask if she knew whether or not Athalia had ever spent time in a mental institution.

Arnold inferred there might have been a conspiracy between the reporter and some of the other witnesses but he delayed naming conspirators until final arguments.

Before sitting down, Arnold presented a biographical sketch of the defendant. In brief, he said Stanford was born in Atlanta, Georgia, and had attended schools in the state including Emory University where he received a degree in business administration after World War II.

He had married an "Atlanta lady" who became the mother of his three daughters. During the war, Stanford had served in the Merchant Marines, then became a Naval Reserve lieutenant and worked for Fairchild Aircraft Industries in Maryland before coming to St. Augustine. Arnold assured jurors there was no basis for Mrs. Lindsley's criticism of Stanford at County Commission meetings.

"He was a marine engineer, not a civil engineer, and the county commission knew that when they hired him. He was hired as county manager, not county engineer, and Stanford had not used the title of engineer," Arnold added.

He acknowledged that *St. Augustine Record* reporter, Jackie Feagin, "came up with a story" that Mrs. Lindsley once had told commissioners Stanford had threatened her life. Gesturing with outstretched arms, Arnold lamented the fact that Stanford was restrained by the commission from answering that accusation.

After his arrest, Stanford had promised to produce witnesses who could testify that he was at his office at the County Road Department about the same time Mrs. Lindsley was killed five miles away. When the defense portion of the trial began, Ray Fox, owner of a welding works near the jail, was the first to place Stanford at his office near the time Athalia was killed.

(It had been established shortly after the murder that the Stanford office was about six miles north of his home, an estimated 10 to 15 minute drive if one did not exceed speed limits along the route where permitted speeds averaged 30 miles an hour).

Fox testified he passed the county road department offices between five forty-five and six o'clock on the evening of the murder and saw Stanford's blue and white Chevrolet Impala parked out front. In fact, he had passed Stanford's office twice within that 15 minute period. He said the first time he passed, he was on his way to his welding shop to drop off a load of plywood. After dumping the load, he left "to go get a beer" and noticed as he passed the road department office that Stanford's car was still there.

Then, Dixon Stanford, (the name being the same is another weird coincidence) who, at the time of the murder, was a prisoner at the county jail across from the road department office, testified he had seen the county manager's car parked out front of his office at "pretty close to 6:30 p.m." the evening Athalia was killed.

Another witness, Floyd Hardin, testified he had waved to Stanford at a stoplight at the intersection of Riberia and King Street between 6:30 p.m. and 6:45 p.m. the evening of the murder. He said Stanford was headed south on Riberia so Floyd assumed he was on his way home. The intersection was not far from the marsh area where Lee found the weapon and the bag of clothing but that fact was not brought out in the testimony.

Instead, Prosecutor Watson waded in on the fact that Stanford had once helped Floyd get a free place to live in an old house at Lighthouse Park where the light-house keeper had lived when the lighthouse was manually operated.

Hardin said the free rent was in exchange for his repairing the leaky roof and installing air-conditioning at his own expense. However, he admitted under pressure from Watson that he and Stanford were good friends and that he had told him the day after the murder, "If you ever need a witness, I'll help."

Hardin said he had made the offer after going to Stanford's home to ask him if he had killed Mrs. Lindsley.

"Suppose he'd said 'yes'?" Watson asked.

If that had happened, Floyd said he would have gone straight to Sheriff Garrett.

After Hardin left the stand, his sister-in-law, Adelle McLaughlin, was called as what newspapers dubbed "a surprise witness."

Ms. McLaughlin said she got off work at Flagler Hospital around four thirty the afternoon of the murder and rode home on her bicycle, passing Athalia's home on Marine Street between 4:30 and 4:45 p.m. She said she noticed a man in the front yard between the gate to the fence and Mrs. Lindsley's front porch. She said the man appeared to be in his late 50's and had fluffy white hair. She said he was wearing a short-sleeved white shirt and dark trousers. She said the man called, "good afternoon" as she rode by the yard.

"I said, 'hi'," she recalled.

After reading in the newspaper about Mrs. Lindsley's murder, the witness said she decided to tell police about seeing the man. On the afternoon after the murder, she stopped off at the Lindsley house on her way home from work and talked to an officer who was standing in the yard. A report, filed by City Police Officer

Joseph Larrow, confirmed Ms. McLaughlin's story but noted that she had been unable to identify the man.

In court, Ms. McLaughlin explained she did not realize who the man in the yard was until about six months later. After talking to the police, she had gone to see Floyd and his wife, Joyce (her sister). Floyd immediately drove her to the Stanford home and pointed to Stanford who was standing in the front yard. Floyd asked her if Stanford was the man she had seen.

"I told him, 'no, Mr. Stanford was not the man,'" Ms. McLaughlin said.

Finally, she testified that the following July, Hardin had driven her and his wife to the road department and had pointed to a group of men standing out in front, asking if his sister-in-law recognized any of the men.

Ms. McLaughlin said she singled out Dewey Lee, telling Floyd Hardin and her sister that he looked like the man she had seen in Athalia's front yard the afternoon of the murder.

In cross examining the witness, Watson asked if he understood her to say "the man you saw in the yard was wearing a white, short-sleeved shirt?"

"Yes sir," she replied.

"Then, "Watson continued, "If the man who murdered Mrs. Lindsley was wearing a long-sleeved shirt, the murderer could not have been Dewey Lee, now could he?"

Ms. McLaughlin sighed. "I guess not."

During her stint on the stand, Ms. McLaughlin picked Dewey Lee out of a court line-up of five white-haired men which also included County Commission Chairman Herbie Wiles.

Chapter 27

Stanford Takes The Stand

Shortly before noon on the 11th day of the trial, Alan Stanford took the stand, ending the see-sawing speculation over whether defense attorneys would subject him to walking that mental tightrope.

The advantage, of course, was that his willingness to testify might help convince jurors that he was innocent. The disadvantage was the subjecting of himself to exhaustive cross-examination by prosecutors who were prepared with a mile-long list of challenging questions.

If Stanford were riddled by any degree of anxiety, he hid it well. He smiled at the jury before he began in a soft Southern drawl, answering opening questions posed by Arnold. Smooth as high-priced silk, Arnold led Stanford through initial testimony about his background; his feelings about Athalia Lindsley; his movements on the afternoon and evening of the murder; the clothing Dewey

Lee had found in the swamp--the whole ball of wax. You could almost hear the hurried scratching of reporters' pens as Stanford testified there had never been a feud between him and the dead woman. He raised his voice a fraction to say: "I had no feud with anybody."

Stanford swore to having felt more sympathy than anger for Athalia when she attacked him at public meetings. "I didn't like her but I was sympathetic because I thought she was mentally deranged and a lot of people viewed her as a nut."

He most assuredly had not been afraid of losing his job because of her allegations that he was incompetent, he testified, explaining that after the county hired him to supervise the work of the road and bridge department, he immediately began studying for tests that would license him as a civil engineer in Florida. In the interim, he was using the title of county manager rather than that of county engineer.

Stanford admitted he had failed one part of a two-part examination in October of 1973 but he planned to take the test again and, in preparation, began going to Jacksonville once a week to take an evening refresher course in civil engineering. He had attended one of the classes the night before Mrs. Lindsley was murdered.

Stanford sat like a stoic when Arnold began holding up pieces of the bloodstained clothing Dewey Lee had recovered from the swamp. Without showing a trace of emotion, Stanford denied any of the items of clothing were his. He claimed the belt Lee turned in was wider than any of the belts he owned. The shoes looked similar to a pair he owned, but "I still have them," he said.

When Arnold held up the long-sleeved white shirt that bore Stanford's laundry mark, the witness said he owned a dozen or more white shirts but he did not recognize the stained garment as being one of them. Examining the watch in evidence, Stanford said he had lost a similar looking "round Hamilton" but "the band was different." He testified he had not seen his watch since the sheriff's department had searched his home two days after the murder. "I was not at home when the search began. When I arrived, the place was running over with police. When they left, everything was topsy-turvey. It seemed they had searched everything in the house."

Stanford testified he had become "the prime suspect" the day following the murder. "I went to work that morning and received a phone call to report for a conference at the sheriff's office." During that conference, he said Dudley Garrett asked him point blank if he had killed his neighbor, Mrs. Lindsley.

Although he had answered 'no', Stanford said Garrett had informed him: "You're my prime suspect. I will have to put you to some inconvenience."

The inconvenience began with Garrett confiscating the Chevrolet Impala the county furnished Stanford for his job. Garrett also asked him to turn over the clothes he had worn at the office the previous day. Stanford said he gave those clothes to a deputy who drove him home at noon-time.

Arnold then asked him to give a detailed account of his movements the afternoon of the murder, beginning with his arrival home from the office at 5:15 p.m.

Stanford testified that he mixed himself a gin and tonic and then walked through the house to pick up the newspaper in the front yard. After that, he had gone upstairs to change into work clothes and then returned to the kitchen. He said he was standing at the sink when his wife and daughters came home. After that he said he mixed a second drink and got to thinking about some permits the county needed to sink some old liberty ships for the purpose of creating an artificial fishing reef in the Atlantic Ocean near St. Augustine Beach. When he suddenly realized the deadline for mailing off the necessary paperwork had been that day, he decided to skip supper and return to the office. He was not sure if his secretary had mailed the papers and he made a point of never bothering her with calls to her home after work hours. His secretary, Hazel Brown, already had testified that she had not told Stanford she had mailed the papers that afternoon.

Stanford estimated the time was between 5:30 and 5:45 p.m. when he got into the car and drove back to the office. Once he determined the papers had been mailed, he decided to stay at the office and study an engineering text. Returning home about 6:45, he said he learned about the murder from police who were standing in the back yard when his car reached the driveway.

City Police Officer Frances O'Loughlin, who was later elected sheriff of St. Johns County, had testified earlier to Stanford's reaction when he was told about the murder. O'Loughlin said Stanford asked: "Was Mrs. Lindsley shot or cut?" On the stand, Stanford admitted asking that question.

Much of Stanford's testimony was challenged during a grueling cross-examination. State Attorney Boyles tried very hard to establish that Stanford had been very much embroiled in a feud with the dead woman.

"Would you describe your difficulties with Mrs. Lindsley as a feud or a nightmare?" Boyles asked.

"You just described it for me--a difficulty." Stanford replied quickly.

Boyles tried again. "Would you describe the difficulty with the barking dogs, the cutting of trees along the property line (ordered by Mrs. Lindsley) and her appearances before the county commission where she charged you with incompetence, as a nightmare or a feud?"

"I do not describe it as either," Stanford replied.

Stanford testified that at one point he had considered filing a suit to try and get a court order to stop Athalia from criticizing him at public meetings. He also denied with a flicker of agitation that he ever threatened her life or made so much as a veiled threat to anyone, including the reporter, Shannon Smith. He admitted he had called Mrs. Smith at home but the date was earlier than the one the reporter had stated in her testimony. Stanford said the purpose of the call was to ask if Mrs. Lindsley ever had been hospitalized for mental illness or if "Mrs. Smith knew how many times Mrs. Lindsley had been married or the names of her former husbands. I wanted any information she had that might be helpful if I filed a suit but she didn't tell me anything."

Stanford said it was true he had asked Sheriff Garrett to check on whether Athalia had a criminal record. He glared at Boyles when the state attorney began a line of questioning, aimed at getting him to admit he had threatened Athalia's life after failing to uncover information that would discredit her character. Vehemently and repeatedly, he denied ever threatening anyone's life.

Stanford said the county commission chairman had prevented him from answering Athalia when she accused him of threatening to kill her. He repeatedly denied he ever had taken part in quarrels over the dogs, nor was he a party to the suit his wife and the McCormick family had filed. He said it was his wife, not he, who had been upset by the barking.

Adding, "Mrs. Lindsley was keeping about seven dogs and two goats at the time the suit was filed."

Stanford admitted he suspected Athalia's public attacks on him were triggered, in part, by his wife's appearance as a witness at the court hearing that resulted in her having to board two of the dogs and pay a fine.

Boyles pressed on with more questions obviously aimed at trapping the witness into admitting he had been angry enough with Athalia Lindsey to walk across the front yard in broad daylight and hack her to death.

"Wasn't it true," Boyles asked, that Stanford had come home in a rage after two investigators from the Florida Board of Professional Engineers had visited him at his office shortly before the murder, fortified himself with two, maybe three drinks . . . "working up the nerve to kill her?"

"No sir. Absolutely not," Stanford replied icily.

Stanford's testimony about meeting with the state investigators was slightly different from that of the men themselves. He said the investigators told him Athalia Lindsley had initiated a complaint that he was signing documents as a civil engineer. It was no big deal . . . the matter was cleared up after he explained that he used only the title county manager when he signed official documents.

Abruptly, Boyles went to the exhibit table and picked up the wrist watch Dewey Lee testified he found in the swamp near the San Sebastian River. "Is this yours?"

Stanford examined the watch a few seconds and shook his head. He said he could not say it was.

"Are you sure?" Boyles pressed.

"No sir. It looks like the round Hamilton watch I had, but it is so defaced I can't say for sure."

Boyles was successful in eliciting an admission from Stanford that he had once taken a watch that resembled the one Boyles was holding to a jeweler, Charles Tanner, for repairs. (In earlier testimony, Tanner had identified the watch found in the swamp as one Stanford had brought to his store for repair.)

Finally, Boyles held up the alleged murder weapon, asking if Stanford recognized the machete as the one he had borrowed from the road department.

The defendant sighed, patience noticeably wearing thin. "Mr. Boyles, I have seen so many machetes . . . was the marsh machete ever shown to me?"

Later he testified that he had borrowed a machete from the road department in late 1973 to use to prune palms at his home. He said he did not recall the machete having any distinctive marks or nicks, such as the nicks on the weapon recovered from the swamp (and believed to have been made when the murder weapon hit the rail on Athalia's porch).

Stanford insisted the machete he borrowed could not have been in his possession on the night of the murder because he already had returned it to the van at the road department where machetes were stored. "I told Fred Hudnall (a road department employee) I returned the machete but he can't remember."

The interrogation of Alan Stanford ended on Saturday, February 1, 1975. Chief Defense Attorney Arnold had the last crack, asking only three questions.

Had Stanford hacked Athalia Lindsley to death with a machete on January 23, 1974?

Had he ever had a mental problem?

Had he ever been treated by a psychiatrist?

Stanford's reply to all three questions was the same: "NO SIR."

In a final effort to shift suspicion from Stanford to another person, Arnold attempted to introduce letters which he said would "show that Mrs. Lindsley was afraid of her husband at the time of the murder."

The letters were written by Athalia and addressed to her sister, Geraldine Horton, who was living in Honolulu at the time. Eastmoore refused to allow the letters to be submitted as evidence but agreed finally that Arnold could read three passages to the jury.

The passages were lifted from letters dated January 8, 1974 and December 15, 1973. In the earlier letter, Athalia had written: "I've never seen anyone as stupid as he is thick-headed. He's a heavy drinker and therefore his reasoning faculties are impaired . . . Jimmie is a complete leach . . . a complete liar. He lies about protecting his dogs. He lets them run the streets."

The portion from the January 8 letter stated that "Jimmy does not have the keys to the house since I had the cylinders changed on both doors about two weeks ago."

Assistant State Attorney Watson offered strong objections to the jury seeing or hearing any part of the letters. He argued that if Arnold could introduce the letters, prosecutors should be allowed to enter passages also found in letters, "stating that Stanford threatened her life."

Watson called Rosemary McCormick as the final witness, to rebut part of Mrs. Stanford's testimony. Mrs. McCormick said she had gone outside a few minutes after six on the evening of the murder and after seeing Athalia's body on the walkway next door, she had screamed: "Alan." She did not recall screaming Patti Stanford's name as Mrs. Stanford had testified, but it had been Patti, rather than her husband who ran out of the house after she screamed. She said Patti came to the fence where Rosemary was standing and asked: "What on earth happened?"

"I asked her 'where is Alan'?"

Watson asked: "What did she say?"

"She said she did not know." Rosemary McCormick replied.

Chapter 28

Jury Hears Conspiracy Theory

Where was Alan Stanford on the evening of January 23, 1974, when his political antagonist, Athalia Ponsell Lindsley, was hacked to death with at least nine blows of a sharp weapon just a stone's throw from his own front door?

The conflicting testimony of a number of the 50-odd witnesses testifying at the trial left that question wide open to debate as prosecutors and defense attorneys prepared closing arguments. Prosecutors had produced a series of witnesses who could link Stanford with the blood-stained clothing and the watch recovered from the tidal marsh. There was testimony that he had borrowed a machete from the road department and never returned it. Some of the state's expert witnesses could not say for sure that the blood on the clothing matched Athalia's blood type. One witness had said the machete found in the swamp was too corroded with rust and other sediment for laboratory testing. Time and the elements had destroyed possible fingerprints on the machete and chemically altered the stained clothing.

Was it possible that the killer--whoever he might be--not only had looked for an isolated area to dispose of the incriminating evidence, but, knowing the damaging effects of salt water, had deliberately picked a saline swamp? At any rate, the choice of hiding places certainly appeared to have worked in Stanford's favor. Stephen Boyles, the blue-eyed prosecutor who opened the state's arguments, hammered away at the "flaws" in Stanford's alibi and waved the numerous contradictions in the testimony of defense witnesses like red flags at the jury. Boyles implied that some of the witnesses, including Mrs. Stanford, had not told the truth. However, none of the trial witnesses ever were charged with perjury.

Boyles stood before the jury, dressed in a blue and white striped seersucker suit that matched his large, piercing eyes, to begin painting a graphic picture of what he believed actually happened that terrible night Athalia Lindsley lost her life. He pictured Stanford as driving home from the office in a great state of anger following the visit by two men from the state who were investigating a complaint signed by Mrs. Lindsley. Boyles emphasized that the two men testified they had told Stanford he must stop signing county documents as a civil engineer. "Things were closing in," Boyles declared. "Mrs. Lindsley was about to get his job."

Boyles paused, giving jurors time to think about it. Then, he began to review Stanford's testimony. Stanford had come home from the office and poured himself a gin and tonic, understandable after a stressful day. Stanford had admitted to mixing a second drink and in Boyles' version of the story, he "probably had consumed a third drink before looking out the window and spotting Athalia in the yard. With two or three drinks to fortify him, Stanford had gone to the garage, grabbed the machete he had borrowed from the county, and walked over there to her, literally hacking the poor woman to death."

Boyles paused for a second time, watching jurors' expressions for reaction, but their faces were like stone.

"Athalia Ponsell Lindsey had a right to live no matter how much she had antagonized Stanford," Boyles said. "But, NOBODY deserves what SHE GOT," Boyles shouted and pounded the lectern, then paused again before continuing his version of the death scene.

At six o'clock on January 23, 1974, Alan Stanford was so enraged by Athalia's meddling in his life, "he did not care whether he was seen or not when he walked across the yard and began swinging the machete. In his state of mind, he didn't care who saw him," Boyles told the jury, in a strident voice, a decibel softer than a yell. The prosecutor speculated that Stanford had finished off Athalia and was walking around the side of the house when his wife ran out the back door. Mrs. Stanford had testified she ran out when she heard screaming but had not seen anyone, he said.

"If she ran out the back, she had to see the killer coming around the house carrying a machete, dripping with blood. Whom did she see? I tell you she saw her husband--the defendant." Boyles, turned away from the jury box and pointed a finger at Stanford.

Boyles theorized that Stanford had heard Rosemary McCormick calling his name and had told his wife to
go back inside and out the front door to keep Mrs.
McCormick occupied "out front" while he went into the
garage to wash up and change clothes. There had been
testimony there was a sink in an area of the garage
Stanford used as a workshop and that laundry was kept in
the garage. It had been easy enough for Stanford to
remove his blood-splattered clothes without going into the
house; stash them in a plastic bag; wipe and wrap the
machete, and, after re-dressing, using clothes in the
laundry bag before fleeing in the county car to the marsh
a few blocks away, Boyles theorized. It was logical,
Boyles continued, that Stanford would think of the marsh
as a good spot to dump the evidence because he had
testified that he kept his boat at a nearby boatyard.

"He knew where to go, "Boyles said, gesturing
like a maestro, before concluding that Stanford's decision
to murder Athalia Lindsley was not premeditated or "he
wouldn't have hit her so many times or as viciously as he
did."

Jurors sat poker-faced as Boyles cautioned them
to "use your collective common sense, judgement and
reasoning in deciding what evidence to accept and what to
discard."

He said it was only natural for the jurors to have
sympathy for the former county manager's family but he
warned them not to stretch that sympathy "and strain your
mind into eclipses of speculative doubt."

Boyles described Athalia as "a strong-willed
woman" who spoke her piece but was doing nothing more
than exercising her right to free speech when she attacked

Stanford's professional credentials at county commission meetings. Locke McCormick, the young man who had seen the attack on Athalia, was as fair as he could be to both the state and the defendant when he testified "he could not swear Stanford was the murderer," Boyles said.

When Stanford's attorney Arnold's turn came to address the jury, he moved the podium closer to the front of the courtroom, near the witness stand, forcing jurors to turn their backs on the spectators. Boyles had stood where the panelists could, if they chose, shift their eyes back and forth. Arnold knew spectators had mixed opinions about Stanford's guilt. He was taking no chances that anyone would unintentionally or otherwise signal feelings to jurors. Perhaps Arnold had observed spectator reaction while Boyles was waxing on.

Arnold began his arguments by justifying why some of the trial witnesses had given testimony that did not jibe with what they had told investigators a day or so after the murder. He reminded jurors that a year had elapsed since the murder and if testimony differed from statements made 12 months earlier, it was because time played tricks on memory. As one example, Arnold said too much time had passed for the state engineering investigator who testified Stanford was wearing dark blue pants with a red stripe design on the afternoon of the murder to possibly recall how Stanford had been dressed that long ago.

On the heels of giving examples of how time fogs memory, Arnold stressed the importance of the testimony of a defense witness who had described in full detail the appearance of a man she had seen in the yard of the Lindsley home, also a year earlier, on the afternoon of

January 23, 1974. That witness had testified that the man was Dewey Lee, a mechanic for the county road department, who found the machete and the bloody clothing that prosecutors had submitted as evidence at the trial.

Without naming the witness, Arnold used her testimony to suggest that Lee could have murdered Mrs. Lindsley and buried the same items he turned in to the police to collect the $500 reward, and Arnold hinted that Lee could have been hired by former Mayor James Lindsley to do away with his wife, Athalia. Arnold charged prosecutors with failing to present evidence placing Stanford anywhere near the murder scene, contending that "Mrs. Lindsley was either attacked by a maniac or a hired killer."

Lifting his voice slightly, Arnold contended that "THE KILLER was probably in the house and followed Mrs. Lindsley out there and killed her on the front steps." There was no way of actually proving the killer had come from inside the house because the police had failed to dust for fingerprints, Arnold reasoned. Police had found the house unlocked and Athalia's keys in the door. Anyone could have slipped in the back way that afternoon. Arnold addressed the jury a full hour and thirty minutes before Eastmoore recessed court for lunch.

When court resumed that afternoon, Ed Booth, Arnold's assistant, continued defense arguments.

Booth, a former prosecutor, spoke to the jury in a voice, soothing as a lullaby. "The only link in this murder case is Dewey Lee," he declared, leaning on the lectern. He reminded the jury that Dewey Lee had access to the truck where machetes were stored at the county road department. It was Lee who had quickly turned in a corroded weapon, clothing, rags and other items after the offering of a $500 reward. The shirt Lee said he found in the swamp could have been stolen. After all, Mrs. Stanford testified the laundry lost five of her husband's shirts prior to the murder, Booth said.

The attorney then raised the question of why the prosecution had not called for testimony by Lt. Eddie Lightsey, the deputy Lee testified he had called after finding the machete and bag of clothing in the marsh.

Booth had carefully reviewed police records and found that Lightsey had conducted a good part of the investigation for Sheriff Dudley Garrett. "It is common knowledge that Lightsey and Lee were good friends."

Then, Booth made the charge that rang through the quiet courtroom like a clap of thunder. "Lightsey, Lee and former Mayor Lindsley conspired to frame the defendant."

Booth speculated it would have been easy enough for Lt. Lightsey to steal Stanford's watch during the search of the Stanford home just two days after the murder. The offer of the reward money and the discovery of marsh evidence could have been "a concocted situation."

"We could call this case the Lightsey-Lee show, produced by James Lindsley, directed by Eddie Lightsey and starring Dewey Lee," Booth quipped.

Repeatedly questioning why prosecutors had not called Lightsey to the stand, Booth called the investigator "the phantom of this case."

Booth cautioned the jury not to forget Stanford's testimony that he had observed Lightsey and James Lindsley breaking down the back door of Athalia

Lindsley's home several weeks after the murder. The locks had been changed as evidenced by a letter Athalia wrote to her sister. Stanford had been standing at his kitchen window of his home the afternoon Lt. Lightsey and James Lindsley drove into Athalia's back driveway in a St. Johns County sheriff's squad car.

Didn't the jury think it strange, Booth asked, that the reporter who testified against Mr. Stanford was with them when they broke into the house? Why had none of the three been charged with breaking and entering?

It was true Lindsley and Lightsey had broken into the house but it was too late then for the state to call witnesses to explain the situation.

It had happened during the period that James Lindsley was contesting Athalia's new will, leaving the Marine Street house and all of the furnishings to her sister, Geraldine. Geraldine had hired a moving van to transport most of the furnishings to a storage company in Jacksonville shortly after Athalia's funeral. Lindsley wanted to see what, if anything, she had left in the house. He didn't plan to remove anything and had asked Lightsey and Shannon Smith to go along as witnesses. Shannon had agreed because, even at that point, she was planning on writing a book about the murder and welcomed every opportunity to gather material to which other members of the press were not privy.

Lindsley claimed that some of the paintings and the jewelry that had been in the house had belonged to his mother. He'd asked Geraldine to leave his family possessions until litigation was settled. He wanted to see for himself if she had followed his wishes.

Lindsley had two sets of keys to the back door but neither of them would open the lock. He had no trouble convincing Lightsey that "Geraldine must have changed the locks again" in view of her hostility to the sheriff and Lindsley during the investigation. Hence, Lightsey helped Lindsley literally kick the door open. After they inspected the house, removing nothing, they had nailed boards across the back door.

The house had been pretty bare of furnishings. A table or two had been left behind. There was garbage in the kitchen and a wastebasket in an upstairs bedroom that contained a tissue smeared with what looked like dried blood. Lindsley hadn't recalled seeing the tissue when he searched the house with the police the night of the murder. Lightsey made a note to tell the sheriff about it in the event it had been overlooked by police. That didn't seem likely because Geraldine had spent several weeks in the house and had not mentioned finding a bloody tissue. Garrett had eventually learned from Geraldine that she had used the tissue when she cut herself shaving her legs.

It had struck Shannon Smith as eerie that one of the few things left in the house was a cross shaped from palm fronds, like the ones Episcopalians are given to wear on Palm Sunday. It was tacked on the front door, but the shotgun Athalia had kept in the corner by the door had disappeared. That was about it except that while they were there, Lindsley asked Shannon to pick the fruit that was left on a Key lime tree in the back yard. Shannon had completely forgotten the incident until Lindsley was asked about it briefly on cross examination and Stanford later mentioned it during his lengthy testimony. Ironically, none of the 15 reporters who covered the trial had written a line about the so-called break-in.

Booth used the incident as an attempt to give the prosecution another black eye.

Assistant State Attorney Richard Watson retaliated to Booth's arguments with indignation. He began his summation by cautioning jurists "not to be moved" by "the theatrics" of defense attorneys in their efforts "to spook the jury" by shifting suspicion "that cannot be proved from the defendant to innocent persons."

Watson said the defense tried to pin the murder on Dewey Lee by producing a witness who testified that she saw Lee in Athalia's yard at 4:30 the afternoon of the murder.

"That theory was exploded by the testimony of Stanford's secretary." When defense attorneys had called the secretary to the stand to testify that she had forgotten to tell Stanford she had mailed the papers he was concerned about on the night of the murder, she also testified that Lee was at work all day and had not left the road department until five o'clock.

Watson said the defense then attempted to make James Lindsley the prime suspect because of letters the victim had written to her sister, referring to Lindsley as a "leech and a liar." The kind of defense strategy that casts suspicion on witnesses and slurs their character "deters people from coming forward with knowledge of crimes," Watson charged.

Watson then reviewed what he termed as "discrepancies" in answers Stanford had given police officers who questioned him on the night of the murder and his testimony in court. Watson said Stanford originally told Sgt.

Dominic Nicklo that he had worn tan trousers to work on the day Athalia was murdered but had told Sheriff Garrett the next day the pants he wore to work were dark blue.

"Why tan pants?" Watson raised a finger in question.

Watson reasoned that Stanford said "tan" first because his first concern had been that someone had eye witnessed the murder, and noticed that the killer was wearing dark blue trousers. Watson charged that Stanford changed his story when he realized that someone who had seen him at the office that day might recall what he had worn.

The night of the murder, Stanford had told police he had stayed at the office 20 minutes looking for papers that already had been mailed. But, Stanford had changed the length of his stay at the office to 40 minutes because "he found he needed more time to make his alibi stick," Watson said.

Watson recalled how Mrs. Stanford had testified that after viewing the gory murder scene, she had thought a maniac was on the loose.

In that case, Watson argued, why had she not called her husband? Why had she allowed her daughter to take her baby sister outside to swing? Why had she not stopped Patricia from driving off alone to a meeting?

Watson said the answer was simple.

Mrs. Stanford was not afraid "because she knew the identity of the killer."

Chapter 29

Athalia's Curse
Lives On

The murder trial ended in the late afternoon of its 13th day. Jurors were sent from the courtroom to begin deliberations at five minutes past six, about the same time of evening that Athalia Lindsley was murdered. The panelists were tired and hungry and normally would have been escorted to supper before beginning the formidable task facing them. In the interest of saving time, Judge Eastmoore ordered hot supper brought in for jurors to eat while mulling the plethora of evidence.

The courtroom had cleared of spectators. Reporters had scattered, leaving telephone numbers where they could be reached in the unlikely event jurors should arrive at a verdict before they returned. Most of the news gathering crew would write stories to be updated after the verdict was announced.

Stanford and his family disappeared to a sequestered spot, off limits to reporters and known only to Eastmoore and the trial attorneys.

The courthouse was ablaze with lights as bailiffs and other deputies moved about collecting dinner orders from various members of the court who were settled in their offices, preparing for a long vigil. The judge and others were hoping for but not necessarily expecting a midnight verdict. Jurors had a mountain of exhibits to examine. A court reporter was stationed outside the jury room, prepared to re-read any portions of testimony panelists might be confused about.

At 8:30 p.m., Judge Eastmoore had just poured himself a cup of fresh coffee when the phone rang on the desk in chambers. Unbelievably, jurors had reached a verdict. The waiting was over.

Five minutes later the jury's elderly foreman, Jack McDonald, who suffered a fatal heart attack a few weeks later, stood up and handed a piece of folded paper to a bailiff to give to Judge Eastmoore. Tension knifed through the courtroom as Eastmoore, his face a judicial mask, ordered the defendant to rise. Stanford obeyed, his face drained of color.

A moment later he fell to his knees. Jurors had found him "not guilty" or "innocent" as expressed in the press. Then he kissed his wife and his daughters, Patricia and Sherry, his face beaming. He was free to go home with his family, free to pick up the pieces of his life and resume the business of normal living. At that moment he had expected to return to his job with the county but that would not be possible. Commissioners did not all agree restoring his job was the wise thing to do.

The next day newspapers all over Florida and national wire services carried news of the acquittal. Off and on for nearly a week, newspapers carried interviews with Stanford. He told *Miami Herald* reporter Ron Sachs that the fight to prove his innocence had left him heavily in debt. "I was forced to spend my entire life savings and borrow from relatives and friends" . . . a total of $80,000. But, he added, he had every hope county commissioners would take him back as county manager.

In another interview, Stanford said he had been confident the jury would find him innocent because testimony had proven he was a kind of "scapegoat." He said he had been so sure of the verdict, he had prepared a victory statement two days before the trial ended.

In some ways it was a sour victory because the county commission did not restore his job and some former friends were turning a cold shoulder because of some of the evidence prosecutors presented at the trial. As early as the evening of the acquittal, Commissioner Fred Green told Shannon Smith "there is no chance Stanford will be rehired" as county manager. He had won the battle but lost the war, in a sense. Despite the verdict, numerous people in addition to Sheriff Dudley Garrett, Police Sgt. Dominic Nicklo and the majority of the people involved in law enforcement, remained convinced Alan Stanford was guilty. It would seem that Athalia's curse was still with him.

The evening of the acquittal Assistant State Attorney Watson repeatedly refused to comment on the verdict. Finally, to end the continued badgering by the media, he issued a formal statement:

"It would amaze me if anybody could go through that evidence in two and one half hours. I am a firm believer in the jury system and it would be improper for me to comment on the verdict. The case is closed as far as I am concerned."

Sheriff Garrett also told reporters the case was closed. In other words, he would not look for another suspect.

"If I pursued it (the case) further, I would be pursuing an innocent person . . . yes I think he (Stanford) did it." Garrett stated. "I signed the complaint against him and I do not concur with the verdict," Garrett said, lamenting that "you always see some things different you could have done, but if I had been on that jury, I think I could have filled my gaps from the evidence and the testimony."

In a *St. Augustine Record* reporter's post trial interview with Stanford, he said he had survived more than a year of suspicion, accusation, investigation and a 13-day trial "because I have a good family and God . . . I wish you would tell people that if a man has faith in God and confidence in himself, and has a good family, he can make it."

EPILOGUE-1998

Although the acquittal of Alan Stanford technically left the murder of Athalia Lindsley unsolved, law enforcement agencies have made no effort to reopen the case.

In the fall elections following the 1975 murder trial, Sheriff Dudley Garrett was returned to office for another four years in a near landslide election. He continued to insist that he had arrested Athalia's killer and looking elsewhere for suspects would be a waste of time.

City Police Sgt. Francis O'Loughlin, who defeated Garrett in the 1979 race for sheriff, also, left the case in mothballs, because he believed Stanford was guilty.

Neil Perry, current sheriff of St. Johns County, has no plans to take another look at Athalia's murder. Perry was just beginning his career in law enforcement as a part-time deputy at the time of the slaughter.

Testimony at the trial and its outcome did little to change pre-trial opinions regarding Stanford's guilt or innocence. There were also those people without a minim of sympathy for Athalia, who believed she deserved what she got and cared not who wielded the machete.

It is usual from time to time to hear someone recalling the murder investigation as a "comedy of errors" and the trial as a "travesty of justice."

At least one of the jurors who set Stanford free needed reassurance that the panel had handed down the right verdict. The morning after the trial ended, a juror, Charles Rowley, who worked as an exterminator for Florida Pest Control, went directly to the home of Judge Eugene Eastmoore in Palatka. The Eastmoore home was one of the houses Rowley serviced.

The judge was still sleeping when Rowley came to the door and spoke with Eastmoore's wife. Rowley told her the jury had been troubled over the difference in the sizes of the shoes found in the marsh and the shoes Stanford wore at the trial. The discarded pair was a size 9 ½ D. The shoes Stanford wore were size 10 C but the actual difference was only an eighth of an inch.

Six months later, Eastmoore received a call from an insurance company, checking on a claim on a watch Stanford had filed. The company wanted to verify that the watch had been seized as evidence in a murder trial.

Secretaries in the State Attorney's office in St. Augustine reported that Stanford had asked to have the clothes, which were part of the trial evidence, returned to him.

Stanford also asked for his county job back but St. Johns County Commissioners failed to reinstate him for reasons that are not part of any public record.

Commissioner Fred Green made no secret of the fact he had reason to believe Stanford was guilty. On the night of the murder, Green and Locke McCormick's father, Connie, were on a hunting trip in Mexico. Green said he was alone in their motel room when Rosemary McCormick called from St. Augustine. She asked Green to tell her husband to "get home" because Alan Stanford had killed Athalia Lindsley and Locke was an eyewitness.

After a turn-down by the commission, Stanford sold his Marine Street home and moved his family to Miami where he took a job with a biological testing firm.

Several years later the Stanfords moved from Miami to Charleston, South Carolina where he took a job as naval engineer at the Charleston Naval Shipyard. Mrs.

Patricia Mullen Stanford died in 1987, a victim of lung cancer. Stanford remarried and lives in South Carolina.

He has never returned to St. Augustine even for a brief visit but agreed to a telephone interview with the *St. Augustine Record* in 1989 in which he said he had his own theory about who killed Athalia Lindsley but declined to give a name. During his trial, Stanford's lawyers had tried to throw suspicion on James Lindsley and Dewey Lee. Stanford said he did not believe it was Lee "although there was some kind of real collusion about that evidence." (clothing, a watch, a machete, and other items Lee had found in a marsh).

A month after the trial, the Rev. Michael Boss, concerned that his parishioners were divided in their judgement of whether he had erred in permitting the use of the office of Trinity Parish for collection of a defense fund for Stanford, resigned as a priest in the Episcopal Diocese of North Florida. He and his family moved to Charleston where he was offered a position as priest in a small church in a South Carolina Diocese. Then, in 1987, he was restored to the priesthood in Florida and became rector of St. Paul's Episcopal Church in Jacksonville, where he received great love and respect until he was forced to retire because of poor health due to a battle with throat cancer.

The courts divided Athalia's estate between James Lindsley and Athalia's sister, Geraldine Horton, who eventually became the best of friends. Geraldine had been hostile toward Jim before the trial. After reading newspaper accounts of the evidence presented in court, she too became convinced that Sheriff Garrett had arrested the right suspect. She did not immediately return to her home in Honolulu, but stayed in Jacksonville at her daughter's home, frequently traveling to St. Augustine to visit James Lindsley.

Athalia's house was sold to an automobile dealer who cosmetically restored it as one of the showcase homes in the neighborhood, removing from around the front yard, the chain-link fence, so important to Athalia's feelings of security. The bloodstained exterior of the house was covered with fresh coats of white paint, removing all traces of the slaughter. The house is pictured in a recently published book by David Nolan, featuring St. Augustine homes of both historic and architectural interest.

James Lindsley sold his ancient family home on St. George Street and continued to live alone in the Lew Boulevard house overlooking Conch Island until his death in 1980.

Lindsley's St. George Street house has been restored as a palatial, historical residence by Fred and Maggie Patterson who have documented that the first two floors of the three level coquina structure were built before 1700. The Pattersons say it is haunted and the structure is one of several downtown houses featured on a "Ghost Tour" conducted in St. Augustine. Neither the former home of Athalia Lindsley nor the Stanford home, which has been sold twice since the Stanfords moved away, is among the houses on the spooky tour.

Maggie Patterson was the reporter covering the Lindsley trial for the *Ponte Vedra Recorder*.

Judge Eastmoore is retired but still lives in Palatka, Florida. Richard Watson, who became chief justice in the seventh court circuit, also has retired from the criminal justice system. Stephen Boyles is now a judge in the seventh court circuit.

Sheriff Garrett has retired from law enforcement and lives in Crestview, Florida.

Dewey Lee died in St. Augustine in September 1997.

The story of the grisly hacking death of Athalia Lindsley remains unfinished because those who know the truth have remained silent all these years.

One purpose of this book has been to present all the known pieces to the puzzle in a fashion that would stimulate interest in helping to find the missing parts.

Nancy Powell and Jim Mast - 1998

About the authors

Nancy S. Powell, began her newspaper career in 1942 with the *Knoxville News Sentinel.* She was hired as a "copy boy" since all the boys were away at war. Because of the attrition in the male ranks due to the draft she soon found herself with a reporters job and was doing front page by-lined work. She attended the University of Tennessee but did not graduate. In the early 1950s she became a features writer for the *Florida Times Union* in Jacksonville, Florida. In 1965 while living in the Florida Keys she worked as a weekly columnist for the *Key West Citizen* and was a stringer for the *Miami Herald.* She has had stories published in nationally circulated periodicals including *Life* magazine. Upon her return to the Jacksonville area she was appointed the *Florida Times-Union* Bureau Chief for St. Augustine... at the time a position normally reserved for men. She held the position for 14 years until her retirement. She is a true professional journalist.

Jim Mast, is from the old school of journalism with no formal education in the profession. He began his career as a printers' apprentice at the *Palatka Daily News* in 1949. He worked his way through his craft as a printer, and pressroom foreman and into the newsroom. He joined the *New York Times* Company in 1971 as Editor and Publisher of the *Fernandina Beach News-Leader.* His expertise in all areas of printing and publishing led to his appointment in 1981 as a Vice President of Municipal Code Corporation, a legal publishing firm in Tallahassee, Florida. He retired from that position in 1997. He is well known in the publishing and newspaper profession, and is a former member of the Florida Press Association and the Florida Sportswriters Association. His articles have been published in a variety of newspapers, periodicals and military publications. He served 32 years in the Florida Army National Guard and is a retired Sergeant Major. Currently he is a writer, farmer and full-time grandfather.